MORE

"*More* is one of those books that seems to come along exactly when you need it. When you hear Benny Perez's story and understand how much he has been through, you will see how God was preparing him for an even greater miracle. God never gives us more than we can handle. The trials and tribulations we face are all meant to strengthen our faith and character. This book shows that even when it seems the odds are stacked against you, the unending favor of God is not far behind."

Pastor Matthew Barnett, Co-founder of the Dream Center, Los Angeles, California

"In a moment, Benny and Wendy Perez were thrust into the perfect storm. Waves of bad reports came crashing in on their world. But what would seemingly be huge subtractions became miraculous additions in their lives and ministry. Less was indeed more! Even greater, Benny would write this book sharing how we too can see the same results. You'll discover sometimes God calms the storm, sometimes He calms us—sometimes neither—and that the 'perfect storm' actually perfects us! Benny will navigate you through your storm and show you how to turn loss into gain, less into more. You'll learn things don't happen *to* you, but *for* you! Benny is a board member of Champion Network, an affiliation of churches with Joel Osteen/Lakewood Church. Joel and I feel honored to serve alongside this amazingly gifted, passionate, and compassionate man."

Phil Munsey, Pastor, Life Church, Irvine, California
Chairman of Champion Network

"Each of us has a God-infused longing for something more; the problem is, the majority of us don't even know where to begin. This book establishes a clear path to the one and only source of 'more.' Get ready for an exciting journey filled with hard questions and clear answers. Get ready for more."

John Bevere, Messenger International
Speaker and bestselling author of *Relentless* and *The Bait of Satan*

"At some point in our lives, we all come to a dangerous and potentially paralyzing crossroads. We hit a situation or circumstance that sends us reeling, causing us to question everything. And the only thing we can think to do is ask, 'Why?' In *More*, Benny Perez takes readers on a journey through the 'Why?' and into the 'What Now?' And he gives us the tangible realization that the difficulties in life can often be the very things God uses to help us discover the most out of life!"

Ed Young, Founding and Senior Pastor, Fellowship Church
Author of *The New York Times* bestseller *Sexperiment*

"I am pleased to say that I know the man behind this message—and every word of *More* rings true regarding the road that my friends Benny and Wendy Perez have walked these past several years. Learn from their story as they moved from being broken to blessed, overwhelmed to obedient, and tragic to triumphant. This book is a must read for those who want to believe that when the enemy puts a period on your journey, God turns it into a comma as He re-writes the story of your life!"

Obed Martinez, Lead Pastor, Destiny Church, Indio, California
Founder, PassionatePastors.com

"Pain and heartbreak challenge the core of the human soul. The options are simple: Embrace the pain and allow God to give you more of Him, more of life, and more faith, or get resentful, become smaller, and get less. This book will encourage you to realize that God is doing more than you could ever imagine. You will find it impossible to put this book down. You will laugh and you will cry as Benny Perez shares his own journey to finding the God of More when life gives you less. Above all, you will find hope and faith, and you will be transformed."

Ashley Evans, Senior Pastor, Influencers Church (Global)

"This book contains supernatural grace to create something out of nothing. As you read *More*, you will encounter the God who is able to do exceedingly, abundantly more than you have ever prayed or imagined. The words from this life-transforming book will leap off the pages and begin to create a Genesis experience in areas that are empty and void."

Jude Fouquier, Lead Pastor, The City Church, Ventura, California

"Every person in every city across the world has experienced the heartache of loss and wondered, 'What do I do now?' Benny Perez answers both the 'what' and the 'how' to triumph over loss and pain. *More* is more than a book: it's a gateway to rediscover the hope and confidence we all need when life throws us a curveball. You'll never view loss the same again after reading this book!"

Sergio De La Mora, Founder and Pastor, Cornerstone Church, San Diego, California, author of *The Heart Revolution*

"For everyone who has ever cried out to God asking, 'Why?' Benny Perez's new book is a must-read. Few men in ministry today are as genuine and straightforward with their personal challenges as Benny. He's open and real about how it feels when God doesn't show up in your time frame. Whether you're in a storm of life today, or see storm clouds on the horizon, *More* will be a great support and encouragement."

Steve Kelly, Senior Pastor, Wave Church,
Virginia Beach, Virginia

"Benny Perez is one of our nation's leading pastors. He has a heart and passion to see people healed in spirit, soul, and body, in a city where brokenness abounds. His writings on the God of More reveal the heart of Jesus and the miracle power He gives in the midst of the storm. We all face the storms of life. Benny's insights, encouragement, and principles to get through the storm are worth your time to read and apply to your life."

Frank Damazio, Lead Pastor, City Bible Church,
Chairman, Ministers Fellowship International

"Benny Perez's life has been scattered with adversity, suffering, and loss. Through it all, he has discovered the God of More—more peace, more comfort, more grace, and more love. Let his story speak to you as you learn to trust God with the most difficult times."

Craig Groeschel, Senior Pastor of LifeChurch.tv
Author of *Soul Detox: Clean Living in a Contaminated World*

"I'm so glad my friend Benny Perez has written this book. *More* gives a powerful message to the Body of Christ about God's love and grace when you go through times of pain. Benny is someone who has walked this out with God. He discovered God is truly a God of More when life gives you less—and you can discover the same. You must read this book."

Stovall Weems, Lead Pastor, Celebration Church, Jacksonville, Florida

"There are certain special people who are God-ordained to teach the world how to hold on to their God-given dreams. In this generation, one of those people is Benny Perez. In *More*, he shows us all how we can continue to stand firm in our faith, even when it seems like the whole world is shaking. Benny has successfully confronted and overcome many challenges, and his practical and powerful insights will cause you to stand up and to believe God for more, even in the midst of the hardest seasons of your life. This book will change your life!"

Dr. Chris Hill, Senior Pastor, The Potter's House of Denver

"This book is testimony to someone who did not 'leave the train in the middle of a tunnel' but continued to walk, trust, and believe that God was working all things for good, despite the circumstances and storms crashing down around him and his family. *More* is a must read—it will build your 'most precious faith,' strengthen your trust in God's goodness, and encourage you that He is faithful and will see you through to the other side. This book is 'hope in print' and 'encouragement in text'—get ready to have your world rocked. Get ready for more of what God has for your life!"

Jurgen Matthesius, Lead Pastor, C3 Church, San Diego California

"When you are going through impossible circumstances, you don't need spiritual clichés. You need Jesus. I've watched Benny and Wendy Perez go through some of the most difficult trials imaginable, and their faith and fierce reliance on God are nothing short of incredible. *More* is the story of their journey, but it is more than that: it is a call to rest in the sufficiency and reality of Jesus, no matter what."

Judah Smith, Lead Pastor, The City Church,
Seattle, Washington, author of *Jesus Is*

"This is a book that will liberate you and help you go to the next level. It's not a book of theories, but a book that Benny Perez has lived out through his life. I thoroughly recommend it."

Russell Evans, Senior Pastor of Planetshakers City Church,
Melbourne, Australia

"At least once in your life, you'll encounter a challenge that could destroy you. You'll face an obstacle that without supernatural help, you'll never make it through. The new book *More* from Benny Perez is the roadmap through that impossible territory. From the streets of East L.A. to the hard lessons learned in Las Vegas, Benny has stared down the impossible. The dictionary defines 'more' as 'farther, beyond, and above.' If that's where your life needs to be, then buy this book, now. Because the greatest test of your life could be just around the next corner."

Phil Cooke, Filmmaker, Media Consultant
Author of *One Big Thing: Discovering What You Were Born to Do*

"Benny Perez is a man who has been tested by the weight of heavy circumstances and has emerged with deeper faith and integrity. In *More*, you're going to see that God can use even your lowest points to catapult you into His higher purpose for your life."

Steven Furtick, Lead Pastor, Elevation Church
Author of *Sun Stand Still* and *Greater*

"*More* makes you realize that there is no reason to settle for less. Benny Perez's transparency helps us understand that all of us go through life's struggles, but that it's important not to sit—or settle—in any of them. He takes you through the pain and the price of some of life's challenges while still challenging you to believe for more."

Tim Storey, Author and Life Coach

"Now more than ever, I believe our world is watching followers of Jesus. Watching how we win, and watching how we struggle. Watching how we celebrate the mountaintops, and watching how we persevere through the valleys of this life. Benny Perez is a man I tell people to watch. You don't plant a church in Las Vegas without realizing the epic struggle that comes with it. This man can teach us all a few things about keeping our eyes on Jesus, no matter *what* this life throws at us. This book will put strength in your spirit while you fight the good fight of faith."

Carl Lentz, Pastor of Hillsong NYC

"Not only does Benny Perez not shy away from challenges, he thrives in leading in the storms. In other words, Benny is at his best when in the ring. The book you now hold in your hands is a testimony to that. You can't turn the pages fast enough. Benny's battles will draw you in and compel you to crawl into the ring and tag-team with him. You've always wanted *More*, and now you have it in your hands."

Dr. Samuel R. Chand, President,
Samuel R. Chand Consulting
Author of *Cracking Your Church's Culture Code*

MORE

Discovering the God of More
When Life Gives You Less

Benny Perez

Authentic

Cover design by Lookout Design

Manuscript prepared by Rick Killian, www.killiancreative.com

Unless otherwise indicated, Scripture quotations are taken from the NEW KING JAMES VERSION of the Bible. Copyright © 1979, 1980, 1982 by Thomas Nelson, Inc. Used by permission. All rights reserved.

Scripture quotations marked NLT are taken from THE HOLY BIBLE, NEW LIVING TRANSLATION, copyright ©1996. Used by permission of Tyndale House Publishers, Inc., Wheaton, Illinois, 60189. All rights reserved.

The Bible text designated the message is from the The Message: The New Testament, Psalms and Proverbs. Copyright © 1993, 1994, 1995, 1996, 2000, 2001, 2002 by Eugene H. Peterson. All rights reserved. Used by permission of NavPress Publishing Group.

The Bible text designated NIV is from the Holy Bible, New International Version®. Copyright © 1973, 1978, 1984, 2011 by Biblica, Inc.TM Used by permission of Zondervan. All rights reserved worldwide. www.zondervan.com

Scripture quotations identified ESV are from The Holy Bible, English Standard Version® (ESV®), copyright © 2001 by Crossway, a publishing ministry of Good News Publishers. Used by permission. All rights reserved. ESV Text Edition: 2007

Published by Authentic Publishers
188 Front Street, Suite 116-44
Franklin, TN 37064

Authentic Publishers is a division of
Authentic Media, Inc.

Printed in the United States of America

Library of Congress Cataloging-in-Publication Data

Perez, Benny
    More : Discovering the god of more when life gives you less / Benny Perez
    p. cm.

ISBN 978-1-78078-105-1
978-1-78078-205-8 (e-book)

Printed in the United States of America
21 20 19 18 17 16 15 14 13   2 3 4 5 6 7 8 9 10 11 12

To Wendy: my wife, best friend, mother, and pastor. Your faith and love during these last few years has demonstrated God's grace to me, our kids, and our church. I love you and believe that God has More for you! And to my kids, Benjamin, Bella, Benaiah and Bébé. You are the More that God has brought into my life. You are the greatest kids on the planet and I love being your dad.

To My Pastors: Paul, Debbie, Henry, Steven, Rachel, Sean, Mitch, and Mycal, you are the greatest team and I am so honored to be doing life together.

To My Staff: What can I say? You make doing church fun and your love for reaching people is contagious.

To My Church: A pastor could not ask for a more loving, dedicated people than you. You have embraced the God of the More during the most trying season of our lives. Jesus loves you and so do I.

Contents

Contents

Foreword

Benny is no business-as-usual Christian. I have never really seen anyone so hungry to take on things most of the rest of the church has sidelined. Others have looked on Las Vegas as "Sin City," and many nationally known ministers have turned their backs on it as a stop on their itineraries. So what does Benny do? He builds a church there and it thrives. Where other churches emphasize internal programs to attract people in the community, Benny sends his people into the streets of Las Vegas to invite gang members, gamblers, prostitutes, and strippers to come hear the word of God. Then he speaks words of God's amazing grace to them, tells them about the incredible love of God in a way that will leave them crying with laughter, and invites them to come back to their Creator and Father just as they are, letting God begin a work in them that will be the adventure of the rest of their lives.

If I were to pick out just one word to describe the messages I hear Benny deliver, that word would be "honest." Benny Perez pulls no punches, and he is as open about his own successes and failures in pursuing God and trying to get life right as I have ever heard from a speaker. Benny Perez will be the first to admit he is a work in process, but it is a process by which God is not just blessing people in Las Vegas, but tens of thousands around the world through the podcasts of The Church at South Las Vegas, and wherever else Benny is invited to speak. Plus, it seems that even God can't resist showing up to see what Benny will do next, and when He does, everyone is blessed.

The stories and teachings you are about to read from Benny Perez are personal, raw, heartbreaking, and ultimately, if you will stay with them to the end, transformational. They expose the nitty-gritty of following God with passion, humor, and transparency. I have never read a message like this about what life can throw at us in this world. Even better, I have never before come away from a book with the realization of how much *more* God truly provides if we continue to trust and pursue Him.

This message will bless you. I am so excited that you picked it up and are willing to let my good friend, Benny Perez, introduce you to the God who is More!

Jentezen Franklin
Senior pastor of Free Chapel, Gainesville, GA
New York Times *best-selling author of* Fasting

Introduction

What a journey we are about to embark on together. Honestly, reading these pages back to myself, I sometimes wonder how my family and I made it through those heartbreaking circumstances. It was truly God's grace. I know it sounds cheesy right now, because you have yet to experience this story, but looking back it was a lot like that old poem "Footprints in the Sand." That's the one that talks about two sets of footprints side by side, God and me walking through life together. Then the scene changes to only one set, and we think that means we are making the journey alone. However, in the end, God tells us there is only one set of footprints because He is carrying us through. Funny as it sounds, that picture accurately represents our story. The only way I could have made it through was with Him carrying me.

Reflecting on two devastating years of my life, however, just makes the subsequent victories all the more joyous. How could we have ever known God would take what the enemy meant for evil and turn it around for good? But He did, in fact, make it really good!

Grace is a beautiful thing. It's the unearned favor of God. It's God doing for you what you can't do for yourself. Looking back, I don't think I passed some sort of "test of God" and therefore was blessed with buildings, children, and favor—but I do believe God strengthened me, and that now I am enjoying another facet of His grace. In the end, I don't deserve any of it—it's all Him.

He kept me close in every dark moment and continued to surround me in every victorious one. Because *Jesus* began this work, *He* brought me this far, *He* writes the book of my life—*He* will finish it. *He* will fulfill all of His promises. *He* will do it. All I have to do is hang on to *Him*.

Please hear me when I say I write this to encourage you. I'm writing this book for you! If you haven't gone through any storms or difficulties in life, then this book is not for you . . . *yet!* You need to know that you can do this—you can make it. The reality is there were so many moments during those couple of years when I wasn't sure *I* could make it, but others came alongside to support and sustain me, and that enabled me to hang on and believe in a God of more than enough. I hope and pray that's what I can do for you: support you, encourage you, and infuse hope into your situation. Life is not over—His grace is still there. This is not your final chapter. Do not put a period where God puts a comma!

Here comes grace! Here comes *more!*

Benny Perez
Las Vegas, Nevada

Show me Your unfailing love in wonderful ways. By Your mighty power You rescue those who seek refuge from their enemies. Guard me as You would guard Your own eyes. Hide me in the shadow of Your wings.

Psalm 17:7-8 NLT

One

Storm Clouds

The year was 2010, the week before Easter—a big day for any pastor, but as the pastor of a church in Las Vegas, it is the biggest weekend of the year for us and one that can mean the difference between life and death for some in our services. It is a huge opportunity for us to reach out to the community and share the message of Jesus, because Easter is the only day of the year many people even consider going to church.

For a church like ours, visitors might include a wide spectrum: prostitutes, strippers, compulsive gamblers, business owners, drug addicts, doctors, lawyers, and stay-at-home moms. We never know who God will bring through our doors. So we have to be at our best because it is certain there will be individuals who need the saving knowledge of Jesus. We had ten services planned for that weekend, starting on the evening of Good Friday. Everyone on the church staff worked hard to make sure each service would impact the lives of those who attended. We anticipated thousands of people to come through our doors that weekend.

My wife, Wendy, and I have three beautiful children and we were expecting our fourth. My oldest son, BJ, was nine at that time. He earned his first-degree black belt in Tae Kwon Do when he was only seven. He wants to follow in the footsteps of his dad and I am so proud of him. Our second born is named Bella and was five. She's a "bella-rina" who dances and sings all around the house. She is compassionate and loving—and a daddy's girl for sure! Our youngest, Benaiah, was two and a half. He was named after a wild man in the Bible who jumped into a pit on a snowy day and killed a lion. That describes our son to a T! Benaiah doesn't know anyone as a stranger—he's always the life of the party! With all of these fun and diverse personalities already in our household, there was a lot of excitement about having a new baby join our bustling brood.

As the pregnancy entered its fourth month, Wendy was scheduled for an ultrasound that Wednesday before Easter. Since everything had progressed normally, I wasn't planning to go with her, but at the last minute something told me I should. Since the clinic is right across the parking lot from our church offices, there was no reason not to. So I called to say I would meet her and my mother-in-law, Pastor Gini Smith, and walked over just before the appointment.

Just a few seconds after the ultrasound started, the nurse located the baby and told us, "There's the heartbeat." She looked at the monitor. "It's 170—perfectly normal."

I remember catching Wendy's eye. We were both so happy.

The nurse began moving the transducer around to take more measurements, and suddenly a slightly puzzled look crossed her face. "Hmm," she said, "the baby's not moving." She shifted the device around on Wendy's belly. "I think I need to get a different view. The baby must be sleeping. Let me get you some cold water—

that usually wakes 'em up. Then we'll see if we can't get the little guy to roll over."

After Wendy drank the water, the nurse looked closely again, but the baby still wasn't moving.

"Maybe if you get up and walk around a little bit. That usually works."

So Wendy got up and walked around the room.

When she laid back down, the nurse scrutinized the monitor screen yet again. Another puzzled look crossed her face as she stared at the grainy image. I followed her gaze. Now the heart rate read 150.

The nurse sat back for a moment. The screen cleared. Then she checked again. Now the heart rate was at 120. Trying not to look alarmed, the nurse explained, "That's a little unusual, but nothing to worry about. I want to have the doctor look at this, though. Let me call her."

While she paged the OB/GYN, I took Wendy's hand and grinned. *Nothing to worry about,* I thought. *I'm sure the doctor will be able to explain what's going on.*

The doctor came right in. Seeing us, she smiled and said, "There seems to be a little bit of a problem, so let's check and see how the baby is doing."

This time the doctor sat down, took the transducer in hand, and started looking for the baby, watching the screen. I couldn't help but wonder to myself, *It's not a good sign when the doctor has to come in, is it?*

> **I couldn't help but wonder to myself, *It's not a good sign when the doctor has to come in, is it?***

"So, doctor, is everything okay?" I asked.

She didn't answer. Her eyes were fixed on the pictures and readings on the monitor. This time when I looked, the heart rate was at 100.

I took a breath. A lump formed in my throat.

I turned to the monitor again and watched: 90 . . . 70 . . . 50 . . . 30 . . . flat line. Right there in front of us. I had no idea what to do.

I looked at the doctor. The blood had drained from her face. She moved the transducer around again and again. A moment later, she looked at Wendy, then at me, then back at Wendy.

"Mrs. and Mr. Perez, in all my years of being a doctor, I have never—" she paused, doing her best to be professional. "I have never seen a baby expire before my eyes. I'm so sorry. There is nothing we can do."

She paused again and then said the words that every parent dreads . . .

"Your baby is dead."

No Options in Sight

By nature, I am a person who looks at any situation in the best light. Ask Wendy. Any time she brings a concern to me, I always say, "Let's look at all the options. We always have options. We need to stay faith-filled and believe God for the best, no matter what happens."

But facing the loss of that child, I really had no idea what to do. I couldn't see any options. I couldn't see anything positive—unless, of course, God worked a miracle.

That may seem farfetched to you, but you need to understand something about me: I have seen miracles. I have prayed for people, and God has healed them. It may sound a little strange to some people, but to me it is natural. Miracles are just a part of my life. I believe in a God who is *more*—*more* than enough.

When I started as a youth minister in southern California and then moved to the Northwest, God did incredible things. Both of the youth groups I led exploded until they exceeded the size of the adult congregations. In the Northwest we were in a small, mostly rural area north of Seattle, and our services exceeded 700 young people per week. When we planted a church in south Las Vegas in 2003, it experienced explosive growth almost overnight. By the end of the first year, we had grown from about twenty-seven to over 600. We saw hundreds changed by the grace of God.

You might think the growth would've slowed down, but it kept going. We added another 600 people the next year. By the time the church was five years old, we had grown to 2,200 and were seeing thousands begin a relationship with Jesus Christ each year. In 2010, we occupied our own building with land to expand. We believed we were on the verge of another explosion. God continued to do miracles. It was more than we had ever dreamed would happen.

Then that season of miracles seemed to turn. We sat and watched our baby's heartbeat disappear that day, just a few days before Easter, right before we were going to celebrate Jesus being raised from the dead. It was the first thunderclap of a storm that was about to hit both our family and our church.

In hindsight, I realize that the clouds had already been gathering for some time. I would not have imagined how the story would unfold and the pain that would grip my heart in light of those changes. In 2004, my father-in-law, Wendell Smith, a great man of God and respected pastor in the Seattle area, had been diagnosed with multiple myeloma and given three years to live. It is a cancer that literally eats away at your bone marrow, causing incredible pain. However, we were claiming victory as he had now gone five years without any significant symptoms. As 2010 dawned, however, the disease began to tighten its grip into a stranglehold.

That was the year I kept asking God the "Why?" questions. I questioned things I had never questioned before. You know what I'm talking about: the questions people say Christians are never supposed to ask—the questions to which we are supposed to already know the answers, because we believe everything that happens in the universe is supposed to make sense to our human minds. They are the questions that lurk in the dark recesses of our conscience, but we never allow to surface because they have the potential to erode our faith. But sometimes you can't ignore them. They just jump out at you, get in your face, and refuse to be ignored. What do you do when that happens? What do you do

> **They are the questions that have the potential to erode our faith.**

when there seems to be nothing but horrible things happening in every direction and heaven seems to have closed for business? What do you do when life has handed you less and the God of More is seemingly silent? What do you do when you keep asking "Why?" and there is no answer?

For Wendy and me, it was a war of attrition. One little thing here, a little less there, here a setback, there a setback. But the sum total felt like a bomb had been dropped and we were standing in the midst of ground zero itself. I did pretty well at staying positive early on. I believed everything we were facing was just a slight deviation from the incredible trajectory of the growth of our church and the blessings of God on our lives. But then the clouds began to darken all around us as my father-in-law began to suffer more and more. Then, like a ton of bricks falling on our heads, we watched our baby die right before our eyes. I felt so helpless. A dam of sorrow broke in my heart, and there was nothing to do but cry out to heaven, empty-handed and defenseless.

Little did we know what lay ahead. We were only in the first weeks of what I now look back on as the two most painful years of our lives. All that I believed about God was going to be shaken to its foundations. It didn't make sense. It wasn't supposed to happen, at least according to my own finite understanding. Something had to be terribly wrong. I was facing one of my life's greatest trials—the "trial of less." And I did the only thing I knew to do: I prayed and I went to the Bible.

Finding Comfort in Paul's Words

Among many Scriptures I read in those months, I immersed myself in the book of Acts, especially regarding the journey Paul took to Rome as a prisoner (chapters 27 and 28). I began to see a picture of a God who does not keep us out of storms but will keep us *in the midst of* storms. I saw how God doesn't desert us. I came to understand how the greatness of God is not always found in the absence of pain, but always in its presence.

When God said, *"I will never leave you nor forsake you"* (Hebrews 13:5), He was talking about times exactly like the ones I was trying to endure. When He told us to boldly come to Him in prayer so that we would *"find grace to help in time of need"* (Hebrews 4:16), it was because He knew at some points in our lives we would need more of His grace than at other times. When the Bible tells us, *"For the more we suffer for Christ, the more God will shower us with his comfort through Christ"* (2 Corinthians 1:5 NLT), we are reminded that when times get tough, the answer is still the same—it is still in turning to Jesus. Life sometimes gives us "less than," but that does not mean God is "less than." He is always more than enough.

Even when we feel like we lie shattered in a million pieces by the weight of life's inexplicable tragedies, God does not leave us. I understand that now more than ever, after all we have been through. We may be broken, we may have made mistakes, or we may have hardships come completely out of the blue, but we are never alone. God is really more than enough, even if it doesn't feel like it in the moment.

I kept asking, "Why? Why? Why?" And God kept answering, "I'm right here." Each time, I thought, *That's not an answer.* But then I began to realize that it was. I had no idea that in those moments, God was giving me the secret that would shift everything, once I fully understood. Jesus was in the midst of all that I was going through, right

> **I kept asking, "Why? Why? Why?" And God kept answering, "I'm right here."**

there with me, and the real question didn't center on "Why?" but "Who?" When Jesus said, "*I am the way, the truth, and the life*" (John 14:6), He wasn't bragging—He was proclaiming that if we want guidance, an answer, or rejuvenation in body or spirit, He is the one we must come to. It's not a formula. It's not a list of comforting platitudes. It's about meeting the God of the universe— the God of More—face-to-face.

I know this might not make sense to you where you are right now in your own life. I know what it is like to hurt and feel there is no answer to what you are going through. I know what it is like to be at the end of your rope. As you will see in the following pages, I know what it is like to lose hope and feel deep despair—to feel "less than," to feel like maybe you did something wrong to deserve this. But despair is not the end to the story unless we let it be. God has something more for you, and it isn't tragedy—it's joy. There is something beyond the storm. There is a God of more than enough, and it is definitely worth sticking around to experience His abundance. He doesn't always answer the way you think, but He is always *more*.

If you are facing a shattered time in your life—a time of *less*— something that makes you feel like I did that day as the heartbeat of our child went from perfectly fine to flat line, I want you to know there is something more on the other side. There is comfort. There is something beyond the grief. There is a God who not only knows exactly what you are feeling right now and empathizes with where you are, but also already has plans for seeing you through to victory and fullness. He won't just see you through; He will see you end up better than ever if you let Him. No matter what you face, it doesn't change God's promises. No matter what happens, the words found in Jeremiah are still true: *"For I know the thoughts that I think toward you, says the LORD, thoughts of peace and not of evil, to give you a future and a hope"* (29:11).

There is a God of More when life gives you less. The grace we receive is greater than the grief we are walking through. If we are going to make things better for ourselves and those around us, we had better expect some storms to endure and battles to overcome. If you are going to succeed in life, you can't let the weather determine when you will go to work and when you won't. Sometimes you just have to press on through the wind and rain, even when you can't see the shoreline.

As for us, we had entered a stormy period of our lives, but I want you to hear the whole story before I tell you how we came out of it. I want to tell you what we found in the midst of a time of *less*. The same God of More who was with us when it was the worst is the same God who wants to be with you in whatever you are going through. There is a way through. There is grace to help when you need it most. There is something *more* when life wants to give you less, and it is found in the One who promised, *"My purpose is to give* [you] *a rich and satisfying life"* (John 10:10 NLT).

The floods have risen up, O LORD. The floods have roared like thunder; the floods have lifted their pounding waves. But mightier than the violent raging of the seas, mightier than the breakers on the shore—the LORD above is mightier than these!

Psalm 93:3-4 NLT

Two

When the Storm Hits

We were in shock. I was totally numb. But suddenly I had an idea. I was certain I knew what to do.

I knew there was nothing to be said at that moment that would help, but I felt an urgent need to get out of that clinic as quickly as we could. I wanted a change of atmosphere.

Wendy and I drove home in complete silence.

I remember somewhere in it all I thought, *Oh, Lord, this can't be happening again.*

This was Wendy's second miscarriage. A little more than a year before, I was on a trip to speak before a large church in Hawaii. In fact, I was actually on my way back to the hotel after playing a round of golf with friends when she called. I was scheduled to speak that night. When I got the call, I was excited, because I wanted to hear the news about her ultrasound that morning. We were hoping for twins, so I was expecting her to say the ultrasound showed she was indeed carrying two babies. After three healthy pregnancies, neither of us felt it was necessary for me to be there for each checkup. It was business as usual as she entered the second trimester of her pregnancy.

When she called, the first thing she asked me was, "Where are you?"

Being in good spirits, I joked, "I'm in Hawaii."

"No," she said, "where are you right now?"

"I'm in a car going back to the hotel."

"Who's driving?"

"Oh, Stan is driving." (Stan is one of the leading businessmen in our church.)

"I've got something to tell you."

I thought, *All right, is it twins?* "What's going on?"

"The baby is dead."

I said, "What?" She told me again. Right there in the car, I bawled. I couldn't believe it. Stan was so shocked that he pulled over to the side of the road in alarm. It was a wave of grief I had never experienced before. We sat there on the side of the road for a while as I prayed, asked God "Why?" and tried to collect myself.

I didn't really get an answer, but in a few minutes I pulled myself together enough for us to continue on down the road. In the following hours, as we tried to decide what to do next, I remembered the story about King David when his first child with Bathsheba had died. Rather than mourn, he rose from prayer and fasting for the child's recovery, cleaned himself up, and went to worship God in the Tabernacle (see 2 Samuel 12:19-23). When I called Wendy back later, I talked with her concerning what I had read about David, and she and I agreed that returning to Las Vegas immediately was unnecessary. There was nothing I could do for the baby or for her now, but there were still things I could do to honor God on my speaking trip. We decided I should stay and preach that night just as God had called me to do, and then get back to her as soon as I could afterward.

So I went to the service that night and preached. My heart was broken, but God mended other hearts that night. No one in the audience even knew I had just lost a child earlier that day. In fact, it was truly one of my most poignant experiences with the God of More. After the service, I caught the red-eye flight home to be with my family.

> **No one in the audience even knew I had just lost a child earlier that day.**

Picking Up Shattered Pieces

In the months to come, we grieved, but life went on. Around Christmas time, we decided to start trying again for another baby. Soon, Wendy got pregnant again, and we were thrilled. With three healthy, full-term pregnancies, we were certain this miscarriage was an isolated event. We rejoiced at the news of this pregnancy and began to dream of this new baby.

But then we were almost paralyzed after watching as that baby's heart rate went to zero before our very eyes.

As we drove home after the ultrasound that day, a resolution grew in me that I was going to do everything I could not to experience that grief again. God was going to make this time different.

When we got home, I told Wendy, "I'm going to pray. This is Easter weekend—this is resurrection weekend. We'll just believe. We'll go in again tomorrow morning, and we'll discover there's been some mistake. God is going to do something incredible." We set up another ultrasound appointment for the following morning, and I set myself to prayer.

Despite the pressing needs of preparations for Easter weekend, I didn't go back to the church. I went down to my home office, closed the door, and opened my heart to God. I didn't come out to eat. I didn't even come out to sleep that night. I stayed up and prayed, believing God was going to answer and work a miracle. I had faith, because I had seen God move miraculously before. I had seen Him intervene repeatedly for people who called out to Him. In fact, I was really a little excited about going to preach that weekend and being able to tell people about how our baby had been declared clinically dead, but that God had raised him back to life.

As I mentioned earlier, miracles from God are a regular part of my life. One miracle typical of what our church had seen involved a man named Eddie.[1] To look at him, you would have thought he was the picture of health. Eddie is a bodybuilder, but a routine checkup in late 2006, required when his company switched insurance providers, showed that he had a heart murmur. This led to a series of tests to determine just what that meant for him. Doctors discovered that Eddie had genetically inherited heart problems from his father. He had an enlarged heart, defective valves, and other issues that made the doctor remark he was amazed Eddie had lived as long as he had.

The doctor likened Eddie's heart to that of an eighty-year-old man instead of a thirty-two-year-old bodybuilder. The doctor told Eddie he expected him to live no longer than two more years. Because of Eddie's condition, he was advised to get his affairs in order and make sure his loved ones would be taken care of when he was gone. Eddie did that, but he also stood on the Bible's promises for healing.

Over the coming months, Eddie had regular checkups and was given medication to manage his symptoms. These drugs would not heal him; they would only maintain his energy and lifestyle as his heart deteriorated further. But Eddie, his wife, family, and a few of us at the church stood in faith, believing God would move on his behalf.

He was scheduled for surgery to insert a pacemaker. Before the operation, the doctor asked that he have an MRI to assess the present condition of his heart.

When he went in for the MRI in June of 2008, something had changed. The technician conducted the procedure as usual, but after looking at the images, she determined there was a problem, so she decided to repeat the test. Eddie was halfway down the hall on his way out when she called him back. She explained that something was amiss with the MRI and she wanted to do it over. He asked her what the problem was, and she told him he would have to talk with his physician about it.

After a third MRI, Eddie went back to his primary doctor, who said, "What did you do?" Eddie responded, "What do you mean? I haven't done anything unusual since the last time we spoke." The doctor looked at him so oddly that Eddie insisted he tell him what was going on. In response, the doctor showed him images of his heart from the previous visit. In Eddie's words, "It was pretty bad. It looked like chewed-up bubble gum." Then he showed him the three scans the technician had just taken. All three showed a heart in perfect condition.

As they looked at the images of Eddie's new heart, the doctor noticed something. He looked closer, and then placed the film on an illuminated fluorescent display for inspection. "What is that?" he asked, pointing to the image.

Eddie looked and said, "I don't know what you are talking about."

The doctor pointed again. "Right there. It looks like there is a handprint on your heart!"

Incredibly, it appeared that God had placed His hand on Eddie's heart and made it completely new.

We have had many miracles and healings like this in our church. People were healed of cancer. A gang member had a gun fired at his head, but the bullets hit the pavement in front of his feet instead. Emotional healing occurred for people who had been abused as children or suffered kidnapping and rape by sex traffickers. Businessmen had new opportunities arise in response to prayer just when they needed them. Other people, who seemed successful but had deep wounds and troubles, experienced changes they knew could only come

> **Incredibly, it appeared that God had placed His hand on Eddie's heart and made it completely new.**

through God. We were used to seeing God move miraculously in our midst.

God doesn't play favorites. I knew if He had done that for Eddie and these others, He could place His hand on our unborn baby and restore him to life as well. I had seen it happen—and it was going to happen again. When we left for the clinic early the next morning, I was full of hope and faith.

Because of the circumstances, the clinic had agreed to schedule our appointment before normal business hours. Wendy and I went in a back door and made our way to the ultrasound room again. There was an air of expectancy. I read in the faces of the staff that they wanted good news for us. They didn't want to let us down, although I could tell they were apprehensive and perhaps even dubious. I ignored it though. I was standing in faith for a miracle, and I wasn't going to allow myself to get distracted by what others thought.

> ## "I'm sorry, Mr. and Mrs. Perez, there is no heartbeat and no blood flow. There is nothing."

As they started the ultrasound this time, however, there were no readings on the monitors. The baby wasn't moving. There was no heartbeat.

The nurse looked at me with obvious disappointment in her face. "I'm sorry, Mr. and Mrs. Perez, there is no heartbeat and no blood flow. There is nothing."

That wasn't the right answer. It wasn't at all what I was expecting. The only thing I could manage to say was, "Are you sure? Are you really sure?"

"Yes, Mr. Perez."

I was in shock. I couldn't say anything else. And all I could think was, *Why? Why, Lord? Why?*

The Problem with "Why?"

"Why?" is a tough question for human beings. Our minds search for answers and patterns, cause and effect, looking for some way to logically explain things too difficult to accept. For every action, there has to be a motive. For every "punishment," there must be a "crime." We know life isn't fair, but we want the universe to be. In the overall scheme of things, if there is a God, and He is good and just, then we want to understand why this or that happened to us, or to Haiti, New Orleans, New York, or Japan.

When I tell people about the loss of our baby, even though they don't mean to be cold or cruel, sometimes they say things that demonstrate a need to make sense of what happened. I have heard things like, "Well, you didn't have enough faith," or, "Are you sure there wasn't some sin in your life you hadn't confessed?" We want God to make sense on our own terms, and if He doesn't, some people decide to deny the existence of God—or dispute that He is loving, good, and just—because that is the only way to make sense of the world. We are tempted to think that bad things happen to good people only because there is no God to intervene.

I understand why some people take that route. In the course of my life with the illnesses I faced in childhood, my unanswered prayers, turbulent early childhood experiences and family issues, there were times I questioned God and His existence for those same reasons.

Truthfully, I didn't have the best of beginnings. If anyone could feel like life had handed him less, it was me. When I was born, the umbilical cord was wrapped around my neck. Medical personnel rushed me to the ICU, and my mom almost died. My family went through some tumultuous times when I was young. Between my eighth- and ninth-grade years, I was diagnosed with Marfan syndrome (a hereditary condition that attacks the body's structural and connective tissues of the bones, cardiovascular system, eyes, and skin), hyperthyroidism, rheumatoid arthritis, scoliosis, and other ailments. Doctors told me I would be in a wheelchair by the time I was twenty-five. I experienced pain, rejection, and abandonment—each challenge ate away at my faith.

I went to a Christian high school, but even that was rough on a kid with so many things to make him appear "abnormal." As a freshman, I stood four feet, ten inches tall and weighed eighty-five pounds. I was so thin that kids would ask me what concentration camp I had escaped from. I also had Graves' disease, which makes your eyes protrude like Bart Simpson's. Kids used to call me "bug eyes." Yet in spite of this, I went out for the football team. The coaches were so afraid I would get hurt that they kept me on the sideline and asked me not to participate again the following year.

My mom took me to every specialist in Los Angeles, but nothing they did seemed to help. To spur my growth, the doctors put me on Dianabol, one of the earliest steroids. Today, it is outlawed by every professional sport, because of the side effects. With each new doctor we went to, we always felt just one step away from the answer—but that answer never came.

To make matters worse, since the doctors had no answers, my parents took me to every healing evangelist who came to our church. Each time, I would go forward to get prayed for. Some would lay hands on me, some would push me to the ground and claim I was healed. Often they would tell me I was healed, but when I opened my eyes after prayer, I knew it wasn't true. How? Because in addition to all of those diseases, my eyesight is severely impaired in one of my eyes. When I opened my eyes and still couldn't see clearly, I knew nothing had happened.

I struggled. I believed in God from a young age and wondered why He never healed me. I grew more and more bitter each year of high school because of the cards I had been dealt. I was critical, cynical, and caustic. My sarcasm was a main coping mechanism, and because I was funny, I started overcoming some of my social awkwardness.

I was told again and again at church that God was good, but I didn't see how that was possible. He certainly wasn't good to me. I struggled with why God would heal others and not me—or if He was even real. Life seemed unfair, always "less than." If there was no help from God, I had to make life work all on my own. I could not see how pursuing God made any sense when He obviously wasn't anything I had been told He was.

Eventually I wandered away from the church, but I wasn't very proficient at sinning. I went to clubs and bars, but because there had been alcohol and drug abuse in the family, I promised myself I would never drink or take drugs. I didn't sleep around because, simply put, no girl wanted to sleep with a scrawny little bug-eyed kid.

Thus, I seemed to fail both at being good *and* at being bad. I wasn't sure God existed, but wasn't really sure He didn't exist either. The "Whys?" dominated my spiritual life. But answers weren't coming easily. I determined all I could do was go to college, major in a field that would make me money, and get a reliable job.

> **I seemed to fail both at being good *and* at being bad.**

Then, in July of 1986, God got hold of me. While I was trying to avoid God, my dad and mom had told me I could live at home rent-free while enrolled in college if I continued to attend church. I planned to major in accounting, because I was practical about my money, as I still am today. I considered it a great deal to have a place to live for free in exchange for a few hours each Sunday morning. I mean, crunch the numbers—it's a no-brainer.

Of course, living at home also meant I had to put up with my parents' nagging about my spiritual life, so I chose to be out of the house as much as possible. To counter this, my mom waited up to meet me at the door whenever I came in, no matter how late it was. She always used the time to pray for me. She said that God had told her I was going to be a preacher. I just shook my head, told her I was all right, I didn't need her to pray for me, and that I was going to be an accountant. I would never have to worry about a lack of money—I was pursuing the American dream.

In the summer of 1986, I looked ahead to enter my senior year at Cal State Fullerton. In July, the church college group I reluctantly attended held a retreat at San Onofre State Beach. Since lots of pretty girls went to the church, I saw a chance to hang out with them. So I decided to go along, even though I had no interest in the "spiritual" activities that would take place. And of course, when I got there, I was stuck—and there were no bikini-clad girls. Once again, life proved to be unfair!

I endured the morning and evening devotional times Sunday through Wednesday of that week, staying in the back and away from the eyes of the leaders as much as possible. I whispered snide comments to anyone who would listen to see if I could get a laugh. That week, I made one friend, Paul, who saw the whole thing as I did—a waste of time.

However, by the Thursday morning meeting, the speakers' messages were sinking into my heart. I couldn't deny God was working on me. I wanted the world to make sense, but all the pain of my diseases, the bitterness from repeated disappointments with doctors and ministers, and all the rejection and ridicule of high school had taken their toll. Certainly I had found a way to compensate for much of it by being funny. Now people liked to be around me and accepted me, but that wasn't enough. I had to admit my life still lacked something, and

> **But then, right there on the beach in front of hundreds of strangers, God touched my heart.**

every word the leaders spoke that week seemed to make my need more acute and difficult to ignore.

On Thursday afternoon, Paul and I walked on the beach, looking at all the girls, watching people surf, and talking about what the speakers had been saying. We were both viewing it from the outside in—agreeing to come for our own reasons, but not wanting to buy in. I didn't want to believe in God. He certainly wasn't part of my future plans. But then, right there on the beach in front of hundreds of strangers, God touched my heart as we walked and I fell to my knees.

It is hard to explain exactly what that feels like—the best I can do is say it's like being enveloped in love. I wasn't swept up in the emotion of a church service. After all, we were in the middle of a public beach in an environment that had as little to do with God as possible. Yet right in the middle of that, it was as if God wrapped His arms around me. I realized right there that the sum total of my life wasn't the struggles, the pain, the "less," but it was the God who takes all the struggles and adds His love and grace and produces *more* when there was definitely *less*.

I started weeping. Paul, shocked and probably hoping no one noticed, asked what was wrong.

"Paul," I said, "I am away from God and He is calling me back."

Then he fell to his knees and started weeping, too. We knelt there and bawled. I knew people must have been walking by and pointing, but I couldn't help it and in that moment I didn't care.

No longer could I deny God was real. No matter how much I had suffered, there was no more denying that He was good and that He loved me. My whole body seemed to tremble under the weight of that very goodness and love.

As if that hadn't been enough, the leader at the devotional that night called Paul out and gave him a word from God. He "read our mail" just as if he had watched a movie of what had happened to us on the beach earlier that afternoon. I started bawling again. Then as the leader started to sit down, he stopped, got back up, and looked at Paul again. "Paul," he said, "you are going to go to Bible college, but you are not going to go alone. Benny Perez is going to go with you."

Days later, I finally worked up the courage to tell my mom and dad what had happened to me—what God had done at the retreat, and that now my plans had changed because God was calling me into the ministry. We sat down to dinner that night and I started, "Mom, Dad, I have to tell you something . . ."

That was as far as I got before my mom interrupted. "Wait. Don't say a word. The Holy Spirit spoke to me at three o'clock in the afternoon today and told me I could share what He told me before you said anything." Then she described nearly everything that happened to me at the retreat just as if she had watched it on screen. I knew no one had told her or my dad what had happened. I dropped my knife and fork in disbelief. My eyes again welled up with tears.

"Benny," she said, and my dad took her hand in agreement, "we bless you. You can leave Cal State Fullerton and enroll at Vanguard University." (Vanguard is a prominent Christian college in nearby Costa Mesa.)

> God heals, He blesses, He wraps people in His love. He is the more in a life of less.

Despite being in my senior year at Cal State Fullerton, that's what I did. I started college all over again, but this time not according to my plans, but according to God's. My life has never been the same since.

A Painful Easter

In the years to come as a youth leader, a traveling preacher, and then a pastor in Las Vegas, I have witnessed incredible things. I know God is real, and everything I have seen Him do is more than I can imagine. God heals, He blesses, He wraps people in His love. He is the more in a life of less. He tells us He knows what we have been through and He wants us to come home to Him, despite anything and everything we have ever done or that has been done to us. He tells us how we are infinitely worth more to Him, despite how we may feel about ourselves. This is the God I preach about. This is the God I serve. This is the God of grace and mercy, the God of More.

Years later, there we were after that second ultrasound appointment, literally going home with our hearts in pieces. It was almost our biggest weekend yet as a church, with Easter just hours away, but a storm had broken over our house and our hearts. The "Why?" questions filled my mind. Was God trying to tell me something?

O LORD, I have so many enemies; so many are against me. So many are saying, "God will never rescue him!" But You, O LORD, are a shield around me; You are my glory and the One who holds my head high.

Psalm 3:1-3 NLT

Three

Feeling the Full Fury

Before we left the clinic that Thursday, we scheduled a "D and C" (dilation and curettage) for the next morning—ironically, Good Friday. It was easier to keep busy with all that needed to be done before that weekend, and not think too much about what had happened. Personally, I was trying to put grieving off until later. It would have to wait until after Easter.

Friday morning, we showed up at the surgery center still numb from the shock of everything. Normally this procedure takes about twenty minutes, and afterward, the woman is released to recover at home. There is some soreness, but most women are active again the same day.

However, when the hour was up and I hadn't heard anything, I began to wonder what was happening. At an hour and a half, I started to get concerned. At two hours, I was worried and couldn't wait any longer. I went to a nurse and, as patiently as I could, asked,

More

"Excuse me, but my wife's in surgery and should have been out by now. Can you tell me what is going on?"

The nurse said she would check, but no one got back to me. Every minute, I grew more concerned that something had gone wrong. Frustrated, I finally insisted, "Look, this is taking too long. You need to get a nurse or someone to go in there and find out what is happening. I need to know what is wrong." All I could do while waiting was pace and pray.

Finally, a nurse came out and told me that there had been some issues during the procedure but that the doctor had taken care of them and my wife was now in the recovery room. I could go back and see her. She couldn't tell me exactly what the issues had been, but I didn't want to waste any more time asking questions before I went back to see Wendy.

She was groggy and incoherent. After trying to talk with her a bit, I asked to see the doctor but was told he had another appointment and was already gone. I wasn't really sure what to make of that, but I wanted to get Wendy home so she could be more comfortable and rest in our own bed. After checking out, we got her into the car and headed home.

On the way, Wendy seemed "out of it" and couldn't hold a steady conversation with me. One thing she was able to tell me was that she was bleeding, but that the doctor had said to expect that. I thought the bleeding seemed a little heavy, but I was so focused on driving that I didn't give it a second thought. Little did I know at the time, but Wendy wasn't just groggy, she was actually going in and out of consciousness.

As I pulled into the driveway, I asked if she wanted me to take her to the couch to rest, or to our bedroom.

Firmly she said, "I want to go to my bedroom."

So I came around to the passenger's side of the car, opened the door, and took her by the arm to support her. We walked through the garage and into the house. As we passed by the garbage cans, Wendy went completely limp. It was so sudden that I didn't have time to do anything except make sure her head didn't hit the pavement. I saw her eyes roll back in her head. We tumbled into the trashcans, and she fell to the floor like a ragdoll.

"Wendy! Wendy!" I called to her, but there was no response.

Then I saw it . . . a pool of blood spreading across the garage floor.

I reached for my cell phone to call 9-1-1, but not finding it in my pocket I ran to get the landline handset, dialing as I came back. I cried out, "Oh my God! Oh my God! Oh my God!" I prayed with everything I had in me.

> **It was so sudden that I didn't have time to do anything except make sure her head didn't hit the pavement.**

I told the 9-1-1 operator that my wife had collapsed, we had just come from surgery, and she was bleeding all over the garage floor. In the midst of that, I spotted my cell phone next to the pool of blood, lying face up. It must have fallen from my pocket when Wendy crumpled. The phone was ringing. I saw the call was from Chris Hill, a close friend and the pastor of The Potter's House in Denver. Knowing I couldn't answer it, I thought, *Lord, just let him pray!*

"Sir," the operator's voice said in my ear, "talk to her. Don't let her lose consciousness. Keep her awake."

"Wendy, Wendy," I pleaded, "stay with me. The paramedics are on their way. It's going to be all right, honey. Talk to me."

She looked back, but her eyes went in and out of focus. I clutched her close to me and kept jabbering. I tried to stay locked onto her eyes and ignore how much the pool of blood had grown while we waited for the ambulance.

The paramedics arrived in about three minutes, but all time was lost to me in what seemed like an eternity of pleading with her to stay alive.

The EMTs went right to work, stopping the bleeding and asking me questions about what had happened. As I answered as best I could, I saw them trying to start an IV, but her blood pressure was so low they couldn't find a vein.

"Sir," one of the paramedics said, interrupting another who was asking me questions, "we're going to take her to the hospital *right now.*"

"Go! Yes, go! Don't worry about me. I'll follow as quickly as I can."

They rushed Wendy to the hospital while I trailed behind.

Split Decisions, A Life in the Balance

We found out later what actually transpired next: In the seconds between the ambulance's arrival at the hospital and a doctor starting a transfusion, any number of things could have happened that would have caused either permanent brain damage or death. Timing was of the essence. Had things been delayed only a matter of minutes, I could have lost both our baby and my wife in just a few short days—and I would have been there, both times, helplessly watching their hearts flat line.

However, by the grace of God, the doctor who met the paramedics at Wendy's gurney had an arterial ultrasound machine cart with him. Using it, he was able to direct the EMTs to find her artery and get an IV started.

In the subsequent hours, medical personnel transfused blood into Wendy's body. I don't know how much blood she had lost, but the doctors told me that if I had gotten her to our bedroom and she had gone to sleep, she would probably never have woken up.

Wendy's condition finally stabilized. It was mid-afternoon by then. She had been moved into a room, her mom had arrived, and I was supposed to preach a Good Friday sermon in just a few hours, the first of ten sermons that weekend. I didn't think I could do it. I didn't want to leave her. I told her I would ask someone else to preach while I stayed with her.

"I'm not going anywhere," I insisted.

She would have none of that. She told me, "Benny, my mom is here. I'm stable. There is nothing you can do. Go preach the hell out of those people!"

I knew she was right, but emotionally I was a wreck. In fact, at that point she may have been better off psychologically than I was. Outside her room, my amazing father-in-law hugged me and said,

> **"There is nothing you can do. Go preach the hell out of those people!"**

"I know what you are going through." Then he looked me in the eyes and said, "Son, go preach!" I wept in his arms. When I was able to collect myself, I went to my office to get myself ready to speak that evening, and when I put my head down on my desk with my hands folded to pray, I burst out in tears again. It had been the toughest few days of my life.

I grabbed my Bible. It was opened to the book of Psalms. I began to read and reread. I turned to various translations and read different Psalms over and over again in each different Bible. One passage that stuck out to me was in Psalm 62:

I wait quietly before God,
   for my victory comes from him.
He alone is my rock and my salvation,
   my fortress where I will never be shaken.

So many enemies against one man—
   all of them trying to kill me.
To them I'm just a broken-down wall
   or a tottering fence.
They plan to topple me from my high position.
   They delight in telling lies about me.
They praise me to my face
   but curse me in their hearts.

Let all that I am wait quietly before God,
   for my hope is in him.
He alone is my rock and my salvation,
   my fortress where I will not be shaken.
My victory and honor come from God alone.
   He is my refuge, a rock where no enemy can reach me.
O my people, trust in him at all times.
   Pour out your heart to him,
   for God is our refuge.

Psalm 62:1-8 NLT

Reading this, I recalled how David had lost a son and had suffered as an outcast and outlaw in his own land because of the jealousy of King Saul (see 2 Samuel 12). Yet through it all, in the midst of his storm, he wrote about God as our rock, salvation, and refuge, where no enemy or storm can reach us. In those few hours, I found that refuge.

And so I preached that night. I preached a message of hope out of grief and loss. In fact, the message of the cross had never been more real to me. I suddenly knew what it was like to lose a child—to give up a son—as God had done when Jesus was crucified. I felt the cost from the Father's perspective for the first time. I felt something of His pain. That night, we held the service mostly by candlelight. Among all the candles was a single red one I had lit in commemoration of our lost children.

> **I suddenly knew what it was like to lose a child—to give up a son—as God had done when Jesus was crucified.**

Before going home, I stopped at the hospital to visit Wendy. When she was ready to go to sleep, I left. I drove back to the house. As I pulled into the garage, I saw the stain of Wendy's blood still on the garage floor next to the trashcans. My emotions were frayed and raw. I had been only minutes from losing the person I loved most in this world. I felt overwhelmed.

How could I know that this was but another storm front in a series due to slam into my life?

A Time for Asking "Why?"

In the weeks following these events, my quiet times of prayer and Bible reading changed. As a pastor, I pray a lot for others, my church, and my family, and read the Bible, all as part of my daily devotions. Now, however, I wanted answers. I needed God to address my "Why?" questions.

Despite my years of bitterness and anger in high school and college, I grew up hearing the stories of the Bible. As a kid, we used to

play the usual Bible trivia games and have Scripture memory contests in Sunday School. We typically focused on the verses that held
promises. We were big on the Bible characters who had achieved
great victories, such as David and Goliath, Samson and the
Philistines, Moses and Pharaoh.

Sometimes the characters in the Bible seemed to resemble comic
book superheroes. These were unbeatable men and women who
couldn't be kept down because they had some kind of special power
or ability from God. They sang the praises of God and worshipped
the One True Creator of the universe who saw them through victory after victory. The good guys always won. God always saved the
day. You could see why they would trust in Him.

Yet, as I read their stories now, I realized these men and women
weren't part of some league of superheroes. They were human
beings. They experienced life, just as we do, with its ups and downs,
setbacks and triumphs, times of loss and "less than." Sure, they won
in the end, but the journey to that end was often rougher than I had
remembered. Victories are not won without battles, and many of
those people suffered defeats, hardships, and trials before they
achieved their ultimate victory.

I began to see that these men and women had to walk through
life just as we do and that they must have had their own "Why?" and
"How come?" questions along the way. I could relate to these
heroes in a way I never had before.

Think of the apostle Paul, for example. His encounter with
Jesus for the first time had some similarities to what happened to
me on the beach at San Onofre. As we read in Acts 9, Paul was on
his way to Damascus with warrants to imprison anyone who was
a follower of Jesus. He was basically a bounty hunter. Legalistic
about his Jewish faith, Paul was certain that all who followed Jesus
were up to no good, causing confusion, and deceptively leading

people away from their Jewish roots. In his mind, Jesus-followers were criminals.

As I have experienced in my own life, with legalism comes bitterness, anger, and cynicism. For Paul, legalism made him zealous and vengeful. He threw people into prison, saw them beaten, and even held the coats of the men who stoned Stephen to death so they wouldn't get blood spattered on their nice clothes. He terrorized anyone who was a follower of Christ.

In the midst of that misguided passion, Paul traveled the road to Damascus, anxious to mind everybody else's business. Just then, God dropped him to the ground. He enveloped Paul in His light and love; Paul's entire world was rotated 180 degrees. His belief system had been upside down and was suddenly turned right-side-up. It was as if Paul suddenly took a great gulp of air without realizing he had been holding his breath. There was no more living life as he had lived it before. God had other plans for him. Things changed as he came face to face with God's grace.

Paul went from being one of the greatest opponents of following Jesus to one of His greatest advocates. God empowered and inspired him to write at least two-thirds of the New Testament. Most of what we understand about the way we should do church, the doctrines of grace and faith, and how to walk in the gifts and guidance of the Holy Spirit come from the Scriptures that the Holy Spirit inspired Paul to write.

Just as God had done with my mom, He spoke to a man named Ananias and told him everything that had happened to Paul on the road to Damascus. Ananias prayed for Paul, God healed Paul's physical and spiritual blindness, and Paul was ushered into his new life as a minster of Jesus to the people he formerly had persecuted. It was very much like me receiving my mom and dad's blessing to go to Bible college. Old plans passed away; everything became new.

Believe me, I am not trying to compare myself to the apostle Paul, but I am equating "Paul the man" with "Benny the man." I am saying that Paul was just a man like any one of us on a path that is destructive to ourselves and to others. He was caught on the road of religion—thinking he was making himself right with God through his actions and legalism—but then became unmistakably gripped by God's grace. There wasn't anything special about the apostle Paul other than he had met Jesus. There is nothing special about me other than I have met Jesus. If I am less, then Jesus is more!

> **There wasn't anything special about the apostle Paul other than he had met Jesus.**

God's grace has a way of redirecting us. A lot of people think of grace as mainly being forgiveness and acceptance. Others go so far as confusing it with tolerance, arguing the same way some argued to Paul that if grace was such a great thing, why not sin more so that more grace could abound? These are gross misunderstandings of what grace really is because when you encounter real grace as Paul did on the road to Damascus, your inclination is not to sin more, but to respond and live more on fire for God. Grace is the more when you feel less.

Dodging Bullets, Finding Faith

One of our church members used to be in a gang in South Central L.A. As he grew older, he encountered more and more violence, and though he wanted to leave that lifestyle, it looked like the only way out would be via a slab in the police morgue. During one encounter, someone pulled a gun, aimed it point blank at his head, and fired two shots. He grabbed his face . . . searching for the wound to stanch the blood flow . . . but there was none.

One of his friends pulled him aside, looked him over, and saw that his face was fine. There was, however, a little bleeding from one of his legs. Then the friend exclaimed, "Look at the ground where you were standing!" Right there where he had been standing were two bullet holes in the pavement. One of the bullets had kicked up a piece of asphalt, which had hit his leg and caused the bleeding. That was some serious grace!

His reaction to almost dying may surprise you. It wasn't, "Wow! That was close, but I got away with it!" No, his response was, "Why did God do that? I don't deserve to be spared. But now I have another chance. I need to get right with God." Grace is ruthless toward the pain and sin that is in our lives—it is God coming in and making up the difference between who we are and who God has always wanted us to be.

> **Grace is none other than Jesus Himself coming into your life and making it His own.**

Certainly, grace is unmerited favor and the forgiveness of sins through what Jesus did on the cross, but it is more too. It is not just compensation for our sins, but it's also power, wisdom, and unmerited respect that reshapes us into who God wants us to be. Grace prevails over abuse, drug and alcohol addictions, sorrow and loss, feelings of worthlessness, and suicidal thoughts. Grace is none other than Jesus Himself coming into your life and making it His own. It is an overpowering process of transformation and purpose and *more*.

It is why Paul, in the midst of his trials, could say, "*So now I am glad to boast about my weaknesses, so that the power of Christ can work through me*" because God had told him, "*My grace is all you need. My power works best in weakness*" (2 Corinthians 12:9 NLT). When we come to the end of ourselves, we have come to the beginning of God. I am less, but He is more.

If you look ahead in Paul's life, you see evidence of grace all the more. Frankly, he suffered things far more devastating than anything I have experienced. Paul was imprisoned, beaten, and even once left for dead by the side of the road. He went through life trying to spread the news of who Jesus is, and he suffered for it.

When you read the book of Acts about what Paul did, you rightfully marvel at it all. He was involved in amazing miracles and adventures. We're inspired when we read about Paul receiving a vision or seeing a community transformed through the message of God's love, but we gloss over the nights he slept in the cold or went hungry or lay in a ditch bleeding to death, having been beaten too badly to move (see Acts 14).

A writer friend of mine once told me that whether a story is a comedy or a tragedy all depends on where you end it. The apostle Paul refused to let his story end in the ditch. He even got up from there and went back to the very people who tried to kill him to share the love and forgiveness found in knowing Jesus. That's some pretty potent grace. Despite what they had done, and knowing where he himself had come from, he could do nothing else but reach out to them with the love that had transformed his own life. Paul was moving through it—he wasn't stopping and setting up camp there. His story wasn't over yet. He was rewriting what looked like a tragedy and was searching for a better ending. He was hungry for more.

In Acts 27, we find Paul in the midst of a storm that threatened to sink the ship he was aboard. Taken prisoner in the same way he had once taken others prisoner, he was put on trial as a religious dissident. The Jewish officials demanded he be executed.

When Roman justice seemed too slow for them, they planned to ambush a transport that was moving Paul from one prison to another in the hope of murdering him. The Romans, however, sent nearly five hundred soldiers with him to keep him safe during the journey, so the plot was thwarted. Sometimes God's help will come through the most unexpected source.

As was the law of the day for a Roman citizen, Paul appealed to the supreme court of Rome so he could appear before Caesar to plead his case. Jesus had come to Paul in his prison cell and told him, *"Be of good cheer, Paul; for as you have testified for Me in Jerusalem, so you must also bear witness at Rome"* (Acts 23:11).

Paul would speak before the highest court in the land, but he would go there as a convict with a military escort. His journey from Jerusalem to Rome is the longest story in the book of Acts. By the time we get to Acts 27, Paul has had a vision that the ship would be in danger if it didn't stay in port on the island of Crete and spend the winter there. Not listening to him and hoping to winter farther west in a nicer place, the captain and crew chose to set sail. The decision sent the ship into a great storm.

The Bible promises that God will be with us through the storms of life, not that we will avoid storms. Matthew 5:45 says that God *"makes His sun rise on the evil and on the good, and sends rain on the just and on the unjust."* Even in the famous parable of the houses built on the sand and on the rock, having the right foundation does not keep the house from being hit by the storm.

> **The Bible promises that God will be with us through the storms of life, not that we will avoid storms.**

"Anyone who listens to my teaching and follows it is wise, like a person who builds a house on solid rock. Though the rain comes in torrents and the floodwaters rise and the winds beat against that house, it won't collapse because it is built on bedrock. But anyone who hears my teaching and doesn't obey it is foolish, like a person who builds a house on sand. When the rains and floods come and the winds beat against that house, it will collapse with a mighty crash."

Matthew 7:24-27 NLT

Storms of Every Shape and Color

Storms are equal opportunity destroyers. Storms are unavoidable. They don't care if you are black, white, yellow, red, or brown. Storms don't care about your race or your economic situation. They don't care if you are broke, in debt, or have millions in the bank. They don't care if you have a great marriage and family, are divorced and a single parent, can't have kids, have kids out of wedlock, or can't seem to keep a girlfriend or boyfriend. Storms just happen. Storms will come to everyone.

It could be an emotional, relational, physical, or financial storm—it doesn't matter, they just come. The presence of a storm doesn't mean God is angry at you or that you have some secret sin in your life. You can be right in the center of God's will like Paul was, living holy, visited by angels, and receiving visions from heaven—the storm will still crash against your door. One way or the other, you have a choice to make. You can bemoan the cause of the storm, debating whose fault it is, or you can move on to safety. Life sometimes gives you less, but only you determine your response.

Just like Paul, my family and I were hit by a storm. As the grief and fear rocked me, I couldn't honestly say there was something I had done, or forgot to do, that had caused the weather to change in our lives. Even if I had screwed up in some major way and everything that happened was really my fault, the result would have been the same.

I first got a glimpse of this when I read the story of Jesus raising Lazarus from the dead. Jesus traveled to meet Lazarus's sisters, Mary and Martha, shortly after Lazarus had died. He could have arrived before Lazarus died, but He chose to wait. He knew that He was going to raise Lazarus from the dead when He got there. He even told Martha, *"Your brother will rise again"* (John 11:23). He seemed rather matter-of-fact in His response when she said she knew he would one day live again at the resurrection of the righteous:

> "I am the resurrection and the life. He who believes in Me, though he may die, he shall live. And whoever lives and believes in Me shall never die."
>
> *John 11:25-26*

Then He came to Mary and those with her who wept. Jesus didn't offer any conciliatory words to them, nor did He say they were over-reacting, because He knew He was going to raise Lazarus from the dead in just a few minutes. He didn't try to explain to them that if they had just intervened sooner or done something differently—prayed a certain prayer, had more faith, lived differently in some way—then Lazarus would still be alive. Instead we are told in the shortest—and in many ways the most powerful—verse in the Bible, *"Jesus wept"* (John 11:35).

In that moment, in that darkest point before the dawn, the important thing was not an explanation, but an assurance that Jesus was there with Mary. He felt her pain. He cared. He empathized. He was as willing as God in all His glory—and as a man in all his humanness—to kneel down with her in her most painful moment and weep with her.

When I think back on how we watched our baby die—and how close I had come to losing my wife—my eyes still well up with tears. That pain is still extremely close to the surface for me. But to know that there is a God who will sit with me in those times, who will never leave me no matter what I do, and who grieves in those moments with the same intensity I do—that makes all the difference in the world.

> **The important thing was not an explanation, but an assurance that Jesus was there with Mary.**

As the writer of Hebrews said, *"We do not have a High Priest who cannot sympathize with our weaknesses, but was in all points tempted as we are, yet without sin"* (4:15). God didn't cause these events. He wasn't manipulating circumstances to teach me a lesson. Storms hit, life happens—but Jesus is still there, empathizing with us, refusing to give up on us, and providing grace to help us find victory even in what looks to be the worst of defeats.

The LORD is my strength and shield; I trust Him with all my heart. He helps me and my heart is filled with joy.

Psalm 28:7 NLT

Four

Staying with the Ship

When the housing bubble burst and the recession gripped the economy by 2008, Las Vegas was one of the hardest hit cities in the United States. Before then, our church in south Las Vegas was blessed by phenomenal growth and many of our members were blessed financially —since a significant number were businesspeople involved in real estate and construction. We had a church building worth millions of dollars and land to build on. Then, in a matter of months, our buildings, businesses, and homes lost a third to two-thirds of their value.

People in the congregation were losing their jobs right and left. Several of those who provided the most financial support to the church suddenly faced bankruptcy or foreclosure on their homes and businesses. We were making budget but just holding steady with a campus now worth a third of what we had paid for it. Our balance sheet changed virtually overnight: we went from prosperous and growing, to tight and holding our ground.

It seemed that every week we sat with people in our offices who had been significant financial contributors to the church, weeping as they faced the loss of their businesses or homes. The downturn had decimated their cash flow. After half a decade of an almost fairytale existence, it was hard to believe that anything like this was possible. The financial downturn became the constant backdrop to everything we did in the following years.

Then, in addition to the relentless financial pressure, as we closed in on the holiday season of 2010 my father-in-law's condition began to dramatically worsen. Wendell Smith was a striking man, standing tall at six foot two. He had been an international leader, loved by thousands, and a respected speaker, author, and pastor. A true hero to me, he had never said anything negative or critical. He never questioned what was happening or wasted time asking "Why me?" or complaining about anything. My wife told me that a nurse once asked him to rate his daily pain on a one-to-ten scale, and he calmly replied, "Pretty much about a seven." From watching him, though, we had no idea it was anywhere near that high. At a seven I would probably be crying, but not my father-in-law.

Wendell was tough and didn't want to miss a moment of being with the rest of us. He was also a man who understood the power of faith in a God who heals. We stood with him in faith every day for his complete recovery—and had already seen him beat the three-year life expectancy the doctors had given him.

But the cancer was now manifesting with a vengeance. He needed constant medical care. He and my mother-in-law had moved into our home. I wouldn't have had it any other way. We treasured every minute we got to spend with him.

For those who were with him each hour of the day, like my wife and mother-in-law, it was difficult to detect the change in his condition because it was so gradual. But one day when I came home from work, it was obvious something was wrong. And thank God, we also had a doctor friend from the church who just happened to come over that day. She arrived just minutes before the paramedics and confirmed that action needed to be taken immediately. This is one of the reasons it is so important to have outside voices in our lives as we face difficult times.

One of the paramedics who arrived on scene attended our church and was talking with us as this was happening. "Pastor, don't worry. We're going to take care of Pastor Wendell."

In the following hours, all of the family gathered. Because of our doctor friend, we were able to get a private room and make him as comfortable as possible. She answered whatever questions we had, did everything she could, and counseled us at each step along the way. We are still so grateful to her.

All of the grandkids, family, and close friends were able to come and say their good-byes. When everyone was gathered and had their personal time to speak with my father-in-law, we put on worship music and prayed together. My mother-in-law took her husband's hand and, with tears in her eyes, said, "Wendell, it's okay. You can go home." Each of his children echoed her words. We worshipped, and he finally breathed his last breath.

We were together as a family. We all had a chance to say good-bye, but it was hard to face that he had not been healed in this life, despite our prayers. In Pastor Wendell's own words, "No matter what, we win!" He wasn't suffering anymore and as we mourned, we knew he was rejoicing because he was meeting Jesus face to face.

This happened less than a week before Christmas—an intensely emotional time for all of us. Wendell was a man deeply and dearly loved. We scheduled his home-going service for after the holidays in January. We held it in the Seattle area, where he had pastored a great church for sixteen years and would now be laid to rest. Over five thousand people attended the service, along with many influential ministers. It felt as if we were interring a president or king. You couldn't have asked for more respect to be paid to a great leader and man of God.

As honoring and celebratory as Wendell's passing was, it made for the end to a very tough year. Almost every day in the coming months, I greatly missed his advice and support. We were literally facing a future with one less family member, but at the same time, the God of More would never leave us. We still had the promise of being reunited with our family in heaven.

Pulling on the Grace of God

We know life is marked by milestones, and that there will be both bitter and sweet times—but that can seem cliché when losing someone who has been such a significant part of your life. We may know the phases of grief or the twelve steps to recovery, but that doesn't necessarily make it easier to put one foot in front of the other as we move from one day to the next. We get out of bed and off to work, only to face constant reminders that things have changed and the road immediately ahead is not one we're prepared to travel. To move forward with healing and wholeness, we need more than platitudes—we need solid relationships, both with God and with people who love and support us.

> To move forward with healing and wholeness, we need more than platitudes.

During this daunting and painful time, I found myself pulling on the grace of God like never before to get me through. What's more,

I relied on friends and family who stood with us and encouraged us with their care and love more than their words. And again I found solace in the Scriptures during my devotionals.

The story of Paul in his storm again gave me solace and wisdom for how to move on. I remember reading in Acts 27 how the captain of the ship Paul was on decided to push for one more port before harboring for the winter, the most unpredictable season of weather on the Mediterranean. The decision proved disastrous. Though Paul had warned his shipmates that there would be calamity if they didn't spend the winter where they currently were, they didn't listen.

They thought they could make it to a better port by being cautious, so they tried to stay close to the shore, hoping it would protect them. But the winds they encountered drove them out to sea instead. For days, they tried to fight the great northeaster that hit them in the face and kept them from finding safe harbor.

In the end, the storm had its way. They let the ship run. The winds drove them mercilessly forward and they had no idea where they were heading. Afraid they might run aground on a reef or sandbar on the North African coast, they tossed supplies overboard to let the ship ride higher. For more than a week, they saw neither sun nor **Paul did what he knew to do. He prayed.** stars until it must have seemed like they had lived in that storm their entire lives. After two weeks, as the food and water rations were nearing an end, everyone lost hope of being saved.

Everyone, that is, except for Paul. While the rest of the 276 crewmembers and passengers were giving in to despair, Paul did what he knew to do. He prayed. He clung to the word God had given him that he must stand before Caesar. If it were true, then there was no way he could die in this storm. He would have to see Rome first. And he didn't just cling to that word for his own rescue—he asked God to save all those with him as well. Even in a dark hour, Paul was a man of purpose and compassion for others. He was determined not to come out of that storm alone.

Spending the time in prayer rather than in panic, an angel appeared to Paul and declared that although the ship would be lost, every soul on board would come through the storm alive. Again Paul stood before the captain and crew, but this time they were more willing to listen. He told them:

> "But take courage! None of you will lose your lives, even though the ship will go down. For last night an angel of the God to whom I belong and whom I serve stood beside me, and he said, 'Don't be afraid, Paul, for you will surely stand trial before Caesar! What's more, God in his goodness has granted safety to everyone sailing with you.' So take courage! For I believe God. It will be just as he said. But we will be shipwrecked on an island."
>
> *Acts 27:22-26* NLT

The next day, the crew hoisted the mainsail into the wind and made for the shore, hoping to run the ship aground on a beach. Instead, they hit a sandbar some distance still out to sea. The bow of the ship stuck fast. There was no way to dislodge it and try again for shore. Meanwhile, the violent sea began to rip the rear of the ship to pieces. It is one thing to be in the middle of a storm on a boat, but it is quite another to be in the middle of a storm on a boat that is breaking apart.

All onboard realized they had to abandon ship. Since there were other prisoners besides Paul, the Roman soldiers decided to kill them rather than risking escape. However, the centurion in charge of Paul, knowing how valuable he had been in saving their lives, ordered the soldiers to let the prisoners live. He commanded those prisoners who could swim to make for the shoreline, while those too injured or exhausted to swim should try to float to shore, clinging to parts of the wrecked ship.

Clinging to the "Ships of Faith"

As my father-in-law had neared death—something we had been praying against fervently—there were points at which I felt I was too tired to keep swimming. But as I read about Paul's journey in the midst of this storm, I realized that when you are struggling to keep your head above water, you have to hang on to parts of the ship if you are going to make it to shore. Further, it is not enough to just hang on, but you have to know where you are going as well. You can't just float aimlessly—you have to head for the beach.

Through the community of faith called the local church, God provides parts of the "ship" for us to hang on to—while our beachhead remains the Rock, Jesus. That means you must cling to the "ships" God has given you to see you through, the very things God has provided to each of us as a means of knowing His Son. You have to hang on to disciple*ship*. You have to hang on to wor*ship*. You have to hang on to steward*ship*. You have to hang on to fellow*ship*. Maybe those don't seem like big things to you, but when you face big problems, it is the little disciplines that

> God provides parts of the "ship" for us to hang on to—while our beachhead remains the Rock, Jesus.

carry you through. You have to hang on to parts of the ship and keep kicking your feet to head for shore.

If you came to my church, you would probably hear me preach messages that talk about the hope we have in following Jesus. God is a God of blessings. He is a God who keeps His promises. He is the Creator of all who always wants the best for you. What you'd never hear me preach is that following Jesus will mean the end of your suffering, bad situations, or challenges in life. Being a Christian doesn't preclude you from having to live and survive in a fallen world. It doesn't keep you out of life's storms. It just means you won't go through them alone.

> **Being a Christian doesn't keep you out of life's storms. It just means you won't go through them alone.**

You aren't without help—you have the God of More on your side—and by God's grace, you will make it through if you keep yourself focused on seeking Him no matter what adversities rain down upon you. You may have even caused the storm yourself, but it doesn't matter. In any storm, there is only one safe harbor: Jesus. The storms will be different and for different reasons, but *"Jesus Christ is the same yesterday, today, and forever"* (Hebrews 13:8).

As we read in this story, here was the apostle Paul, a man of faith and miracles, and he was right where God had told him to be—on the way to Rome to appear before Caesar. He was walking right in the middle of his divine destiny. And yet, we see him in the middle of a storm on a ship being torn to pieces by raging seas with Roman soldiers debating whether or not to execute him. Believe me, when I read this within weeks of my father-in-law's death, and also remembering what had happened the week of

Easter, it redefined for me what it meant to be between a rock and a hard place.

I drew strength as I remembered how good God had been to us. When we first moved to Las Vegas, it was as if God had paved the way for us to come. We had miraculous events happen one after the other to confirm we were doing just what God called us to do. We were sure we were in His will. We have experienced the blessings and goodness of God in our lives. We know God is good and has more, even when the world keeps giving us less.

The Beginning of an Adventure

When I became a youth pastor back in the early 1990s, I could see God in everything we did. For a short while, I worked in Southern California. Then I received the opportunity to move to the Northwest and become the youth pastor at a church in Marysville, Washington. That was at the height of the grunge movement in Seattle, which meant drugs, partying, and feeling disconnected from family and society.

But in response to God touching hearts in our meetings, kids rejected all of that, often by throwing onto the stage symbols of what they were giving up. We would often collect packs of cigarettes, bags of drugs, syringes, even knives. It wasn't uncommon for people to drive hours to attend these meetings from as far away as Oregon, Montana, or Vancouver, British Columbia. One time, a guy who had been featured on *America's Most Wanted* stumbled into one of our meetings and gave his life to Christ. It was an incredible turnaround. Today, he has finished paying his debt to society and is working as a minister. I know what it is like to see God move.

Around 1998, I began traveling and preaching throughout the country and overseas. I was speaking more than 300 times a year, usually eight to ten times a week. We saw God touch a lot of lives everywhere we went. With so many trips, I sometimes found that Seattle, because of location and weather, can be a tough place to travel from. As a result, in 2001 I started to sense that God wanted us to relocate.

You never want to move a woman from her family without having heard from God.

By this time, Wendy and I had married, and her family was living in the Seattle region where her parents were pastors. You never want to move a woman from her family without having heard from God. So I tucked that feeling away and kept praying.

In the months to come, God's direction became clearer, and we started looking at different cities. We considered moving back east, as well as to the Los Angeles area where I grew up, but nothing felt right. Then I had an opportunity to speak in Las Vegas. Instantly, both Wendy and I liked the city. As we returned to the Northwest, Las Vegas lingered in our minds. Months later, and after much prayer, I asked Wendy if she wanted to take a trip to Vegas to check it out as a place to live. Surprisingly, she agreed.

In the early 2000s, Las Vegas was booming. There were waiting lists for people to buy houses, and businesses were hiring from all over the nation. Finding a development with houses we liked, we decided to visit model homes and get ideas for the future. A man named Guy met us as we got out of the car. He was in charge of model home tours. He didn't mince words, and after greeting us, bluntly said, "I just want to let you know that we have no homes available and there is a waiting list of about two hundred people."

I responded, "That's great. We just wanted to take a look, because my wife likes the architecture and design."

He shrugged. "Well, go right ahead."

So we walked through four homes and decided on the model and location we would like if something were available. Then as we were walking out, the model home guy—Guy—met us again. We thanked him, and he said, "By the way, what model did you like, and what kind of lot would interest you?"

I told him, "You know what, sir, I understand there is a waiting list, so really, it's okay. We just wanted to take a look."

"No, no," he insisted. "Please answer my question."

Surprised by his abruptness, I responded, "Okay, we like the Puccini model, with the loft feature, on a cul-de-sac with a view of the Strip."

He looked at me for a full beat without blinking. Then he said, "This is your lucky day. While you were looking at the models, I got a fax and a deal fell through. Technically, I am supposed to call the first person on this list, but you are here. Do you want to go take a look at the house?"

Not certain what else to say, I answered, "Sure." We got in the car, and Guy drove us to a house in a cul-de-sac that was the Puccini model with the loft build-out that overlooked the Las Vegas Strip. We had to put hard hats on because it was still under construction. The minute Wendy and I stepped onto the property, we started to cry. We knew immediately in our hearts that this was our home and was where God wanted us to live. I just happened to have brought a check with me, so I wrote out the amount of the earnest money, gave it to him, and Wendy and I looked at each other, realizing we were moving to Las Vegas.

We initially had no intention of starting a church in this area, but after living here about a year and traveling all over to have meetings,

I felt God telling me, "What you are doing all over the country, I want you to do in Las Vegas." In obedience, we opened up our house and started to hold meetings. A couple of dozen people came the first time, only two of whom we knew.

After a few months, we had about a hundred people coming, promoting a move to a school auditorium. After praying and seeking God further, we felt He wanted us to start a church. We told the group what we felt the Lord had said, and if they already had a home church, they needed to stay faithful to their pastor and not switch. The next week we had about fifty people, and we grew from there.

In May of 2003, we moved our meetings into a movie theatre, and then in September of that year, we had the official grand opening of The Church at South Las Vegas. Three hundred people came. The following week, two hundred came back, but by the end of the year there were six hundred attending each Sunday. Presently, we have about thirty-two hundred members.

During those years, we lived almost an unbelievably blessed existence. Everywhere we turned, whatever we did flourished. Certainly we had some issues along the way as everyone does, but nothing like what started hitting our lives in 2008, then peaking in 2010 and 2011.

> **I began to see the principles of what we needed to do to make it off the ship and onto the shore.**

We felt strongly we were following God's vision for what He wanted for our lives. We knew we were in His will doing His work, helping people in a city where many feel desperate. But what we began to experience, as the economy tanked, was not the happily-ever-after we had envisioned.

As I continued to read Paul's story in the Bible, I began to see the principles of what we needed to do to make it off the ship and onto the shore. Some we had even been doing without realizing it. We did, in fact, hang on to parts of the ship—we had sought God, and that was sustaining us even more than we had realized.

When difficulties and roadblocks come our way, we have a tendency as human beings to hole up and pull away from others, to isolate, feeling like no one before has ever experienced what we are going through. That little voice in the back of our minds tells us we deserve it. We hear the whispers, such as, "No one cares. You might as well give up." We are often ashamed, whether we have reason to feel that way or not.

Shame is such a toxic emotion that our minds will do almost anything to keep from having to face it. When Adam and Eve disobeyed God, they felt ashamed and tried to hide themselves, first with fig leaves and then in the bush when they heard God walking through the garden to meet them. Without even realizing it, they were separating themselves from the only one who could really help.

When we are ashamed, we pull away from others and isolate ourselves to keep from having to feel guilty or embarrassed about our circumstances. It is so subtle and deceptive that we don't even realize we are doing it. This is exactly how denial, rejection, repression, and other avoidance mechanisms are triggered. We isolate and incubate. Like a wound that never gets properly cleaned, we let things fester.

We think we can handle it—that we can make it on our own. We think things will get better if we just leave them alone. We tell ourselves any number of lies because we don't want to face the shame of not being perfect, as silly as that might sound.

Yet those thoughts are a ploy of the enemy who wants to destroy us. The worst thing we can do when we feel discouraged or distraught is to be alone. This is when many bail out on the house of God, thinking, *God's forsaken me. I'm mad at God. I'm not going to church.* But please understand that church is your lifeline. It's the place you receive hope, faith, and love. It's the place where God grabs hold of you and you believe again. It's where you are renewed—where you are convinced not to give up on what God is doing in your life, even in the midst of a terrible storm.

> **God never intended for us to be alone. That's why the parts of the ship —discipleship, worship, stewardship, and fellowship—are in the church.**

God never intended for us to be alone. That's why the parts of the ship—discipleship, worship, stewardship, and fellowship—are in the church. But it is not just the practices, it is their focus—all of them are intended to help us connect with others and with God. Their ultimate purpose is to connect us with Jesus. It is all about maintaining healthy relationships with God and those who care about you the most.

Without God's grace, I'd be dead. It's why I can acknowledge my weaknesses—because when I am weak, God is strong. When I acknowledge that I need Him, it is then that He can lift me up and use me to help others. It is the main reason I refuse to be embarrassed by my own shortcomings. It is why I openly say that when Wendy and I had difficulties in our marriage, we got counseling. When I'm in a tough situation, I call my pastor friends. When I'm tempted, I go tell my wife. When I don't know what to do, I pray and read my Bible.

I know there is no way I can get through on my own, so I look for parts of the ship to hang on to. God is the more when life is less.

As Proverbs 18:10 says, *"The name of the LORD is a strong tower; the righteous run to it and are safe."*

In the midst of the storm, when Wendy and I were at our lowest, we didn't sleep in or take time off from going to church. We went to church, worshipped God, and spent time talking with friends, even if it was only to talk about basketball or the weather. The need for fellowship and encouragement is why I am grateful for friends like Pastor Jude Fouquier at The City Church in Ventura, California, a fellow sojourner I can call anytime and just open up to.

God brings us together as a community and body for mutual support. After all, He is pulling you through your storm so you can in turn help others make it through theirs. As Paul told the Corinthian believers, *"God is our merciful Father and the source of all comfort. He comforts us in all our troubles so that we can comfort others. When they are troubled, we will be able to give them the same comfort God has given us"* (2 Corinthians 1:3-4 NLT).

That means other people can look at you and say, "If God was there for that person, He will be there for me!" You can be that example. You can be the one pulling on the other side of the lifeline. Paul went on to tell the Corinthians, *"In fact, we expected to die. But as a result, we stopped relying on ourselves and learned to rely only on God, who raises the dead"* (2 Corinthians 1:9 NLT).

If we can be an example of the God of More in situations of *less*, how much *more* will God use what the enemy meant for evil and turn it for good (see Genesis 50:20)?

So in the midst of our storms, we keep paddling onward. We remember the good things God has done for us in the past, the blessings that we've had, and the promises He has given us for our future. We still hurt, and we still want to hide sometimes, but we don't, because there is no healing in isolation. We instead need to hang onto parts of the ship and find our way to shore.

If we are with God and His people, we are closer and closer to getting through the storm, experiencing God's ever-present *more*, and having a testimony of God's faithfulness on the other side.

The voice of the LORD echoes above the sea.
The God of glory thunders.
The LORD thunders over the mighty sea.
The voice of the LORD is powerful;
the voice of the LORD is majestic.

Psalm 29:3-4 NLT

Five

Cold and Rainy

As we were preparing for the home-going service for my father-in-law, the family decided that rather than having flowers sent, we would request donations be given to Rose Hill Cottages, a foster-family housing development Wendell had started as pastor of The City Church in Seattle. Or, people could choose to give to the building fund for our new auditorium, the Dr. Wendell E. Smith Auditorium, in his memory. What we thought was an honoring gesture, as it turned out, started a cascade of dominoes.

As I mentioned, Las Vegas was hit hard by the housing slump and was listed among the highest per capita of foreclosures, home equity loss, and bankruptcies in the United States. Many of our church families faced personal or business foreclosure and/or bankruptcy. Most of the homes owned by our church members lost over 50 percent of their value. Nevada had the highest unemployment rate in the nation during this time. The Las Vegas economy sank dramatically as the tidal wave of defaults swept through the nation.

For the church, this meant the property we had purchased for expansion experienced a 90 percent depreciation. We were over $5 million upside down in our properties, and the experts predicted the property values in the Las Vegas valley wouldn't bounce back until 2032.

> **The experts predicted the property values in the Las Vegas valley wouldn't bounce back until 2032.**

It seemed like when you sit on the beach of the Pacific Ocean and look out over the waves; although you know what the map says, it still looks like the water rolls on without end. That's what we felt like looking at the troubles staring us in the face—there appeared to be no end in sight. It was a hopeless feeling. We questioned whether we had stepped out of the will of God. Did we miss a turn somewhere along the way? Being a pastor, leader, and shepherd, I struggled to know which steps to take and in which direction to head.

Despite the grim forecast, however, we had a plan. Anyone who knows me knows I always need a plan. We wanted to develop the land we owned by building the new auditorium and other facilities, increase the value of our properties, and return our assets-to-debt ratio to a more even keel. In the first weeks of 2011, we were building up cash again to pursue the plan to develop our land. In a situation like this where we felt so stifled and stuck, we felt we had to keep moving forward in any area possible.

Any small step forward at this time was a win. At such a hopeless time in Las Vegas, the church needed to stay a haven and a place of vision. As the Bible makes clear, without vision people live carelessly and often perish (see Proverbs 29:18). Due to the massive disparity between the present worth of our property and the money still owed on the mortgage, we entered into negotiations with the bank, seeking a win-win solution for all parties.

Unfortunately, though, we came to an impasse. We wanted to be the best stewards we could be, but because we were unable to come to a mutually acceptable agreement with the bank, I honestly had no idea what to do.

Experts tell us that stress in our lives is normal, but when one stressful event piles upon another, it can lead to a toxic overdose that can cause a breakdown. The financial upheaval of Las Vegas had been like a slow, relentless dripping faucet for a handful of years; but when you add to that the loss of a child, Wendy's near death, and the passing of my father-in-law in roughly a handful of months, we were nearing a breaking point.

It was as if the crashing violence of the storm we had been experiencing slowed to a steady, cold drizzle that threatened to soak us to the bone mentally, emotionally, and spiritually. It was a dreary, dismal environment, and there was no dawn on the horizon. Left out in the cold, wet to the skin, we were emotionally and mentally shivering.

> **It was as if the crashing violence of the storm we had been experiencing slowed to a steady, cold drizzle.**

Storm on the Horizon

As I continued my study of Paul during his shipwreck and how he led every person on the ship to safety, I noticed an interesting wording of the story in the *New Living Translation* of the Bible. It presents the first verses in Acts 28 in this way:

> Once we were safe on shore, we learned that we were on the island of Malta. The people of the island were very kind to us. *It was cold and rainy*, so they built a fire on the shore to welcome us.
>
> *Acts 28:1-2 NLT (emphasis added)*

Paul and those with him had made it off the ship and onto the shore, but the storm continued. Though they did not experience it as intensely on land as they had at sea, they were already wet and cold from their swim. Once they got out of the water, matters only worsened. I don't know if you have ever been in a cold and rainy environment when you're soaked to the bone and shivering, but it's not a pleasant experience.

They had come out of the sea, been saved from shipwreck, spared execution by the soldiers, and were still far from being safe, warm, fed, and dry. Instead they found themselves out in the open in a place that was cold and rainy; exposed, isolated, exhausted, and susceptible to all of the elements. They were hungry and tired, and still had miles to go before they could rest and eat.

Have you ever experienced a season in your life when no matter what you did, it just didn't seem like you could get either warm or dry?

We thought we had escaped something when 2010 ended, but then came 2011. After the storms of life crashed upon us like a tsunami, we emerged into a time that was more like a steady, cold drizzle we couldn't shake. Have you ever experienced a season in your life when no matter what you did, it just didn't seem like you could get either warm or dry?

You wondered whether you would make it or not, not because something big hit you, but because there was a constant drizzle of bad news soaking you and everything you owned. Maybe at first it seemed like no big deal, but before you knew it, you were soaked to your core. You felt so down and alone, you wondered if you had a future at all.

I know what it is like to be in a cold and rainy environment like this. It reminded me of those old cartoons where the little, black rain cloud follows the guy around, raining on him and nobody else. No matter what he does, he can't shake it. That environment had echoed around the church in a general sense of ill ease as the recession also overshadowed so many of our members, their businesses, their mortgages, and their jobs. Things were tight all around. Where we had once seen incredible growth, we were now just grateful to keep up and stay steady.

Looking back, I see how this season forever changed my measure of success. Even Paul says,

> I have learned in whatever state I am, to be content: I know how to be abased, and I know how to abound. Everywhere and in all things I have learned both to be full and to be hungry, both to abound and to suffer need. I can do all things through Christ who strengthens me.
>
> *Philippians 4:11-13*

After disappointment on top of disappointment, we clung to the simple joys of our family, a marriage that was strong enough to endure, and to the great miracle of hundreds giving their lives to Jesus each month. We were grateful for always coming to the end of the month and not only having enough to make our budget, but also enough to help other local ministries as the economic downturn continued to threaten churches and families throughout the Las Vegas valley.

Perspectives changed, and gratefulness for provision outside of monetary gain prevailed. Generosity toward struggling families—even from families struggling themselves—increased. On several occasions, I felt prompted to stop a worship experience on a weekend and ask if there were families who did not have enough money for food that week. It was not just about embracing them and wishing them the best, nor was it about embarrassing them—I felt compelled to give them the cash out of my pocket.

> I felt prompted to stop a worship experience and ask if there were families who did not have enough money for food that week.

A few hands would be raised, and by the time I had given away the few hundred dollars in my pocket the stage would be littered with hundreds more given by others in the congregation. Thirty- to forty-five minutes later, single parents, families that needed a little extra, even young people left church knowing that God cares about them in a tangible way. (If you want to see some of these experiences, check out the clips at themorebook.com.) This miracle repeated itself on several occasions.

In April of 2011, we held our Easter worship experience called "Easter at the Mack." Rather than have ten services at our building as we had the year before, we rented the University of Nevada at Las Vegas Thomas & Mack Center—the stadium where our major sporting events and concerts take place—to have an Easter weekend for the entire Las Vegas valley.

In conjunction with that, we also had a canned food drive in partnership with a local food bank. We regularly feed and clothe hundreds of people in our community, as well as give to missions and to support other ministries and rehabilitation centers.

With Nevada having the highest unemployment in the nation, there were a lot of people in need of help. We had more than 7,000 people show up, and we were able to donate more than 60,000 pounds of food to those who needed it most. Best of all, we saw more than 1,000 people come forward to give their lives to Jesus. That Easter Sunday, many were taking a positive step out of very negative lifestyles. We reached out to them and built a fire where they could come in from the cold and the rain, and they came by the hundreds.

This is another lesson we can learn from the story of Paul's shipwreck. When everyone finally got off the ship and made it to land, the islanders came to help. They were like the EMTs of that moment—pulling men from the sea, covering them with blankets, and building a fire to warm them. There were no discussions or psychoanalysis of the situation, or guesses of why they were all there. All hands were on deck to save people's lives.

When you are in the midst of a cold and rainy environment, you need to look for the places where someone else is building a fire. In the story of Paul on the island of Malta, those escaping the sea didn't have time to walk back to the village. They were cold and wet, shivering to their bones. So the islanders rescued them and built a fire *where they were*, saving their lives without discrimination.

> **When you are in the midst of a cold and rainy environment, you need to look for the places where someone else is building a fire.**

Problems we face in life have a tendency to isolate us from others because we are ashamed of what we have fallen into. Our minds tell us we are worthless, getting exactly what we deserve, and that no

one else cares. We get so depressed and discouraged that even sui-
cide looks like a better option than facing another day of turmoil.
We meet people who feel that way all of the time.

But that voice in your head is lying to you. You are worth something, there are answers out there, and people do care. In fact, that is
exactly the message of Easter. It is a message of hope. It is the message that you are worth so much that Jesus, the son of God, came to
earth and suffered persecution, torture, and execution on a cross—the
most drastic, painful form of capital punishment ever to exist on the
earth. Why? Because He loves you. Jesus took the epitome of less
upon Himself so that we might freely receive the *more* of His hope.

A High Price—Fully Paid

Whatever mess you have gotten yourself into or has come upon
you, He paid the price to get you out of it on the cross. The debt
has already been paid in full—it's been covered. To Him, you are
worth the sacrifice and suffering He experienced that day. The message of Easter is not only that there
is hope to change, but also that
there is a fire to which you can come
and escape whatever kind of storm
life may be throwing at you.

Being around a fire is comforting.
It's like when we used to have camp-
fires on the beach when I was growing up in California. You sit around
the fire and make s'mores or roast hot dogs. You sit quietly to enjoy
the crackling and dancing of the flames and the sound of the waves
breaking on the shore.

> **Whatever mess you have gotten yourself into, He paid the price to get you out of it on the cross.**

It's a great atmosphere. You feel the warmth against the cold of the night. Then, sometimes, someone will pull out a guitar and start playing. Maybe you'll sing campfire songs. Maybe somebody will tell a story or two. A fire provides warmth. If it is cold and rainy, it provides comfort.

Spiritually speaking, the Bible tells us that God is a consuming fire. There are numerous times in the Bible when God shows up as fire. Take Moses' encounter with God, for example. He was in a cold and rainy part of his life. God had called him to deliver his nation from slavery in Egypt, but Moses messed it up by murdering an Egyptian and found himself exiled (see Exodus 2).

He wandered in the wilderness for forty years, thinking his life was over. Then one day, God showed up. Moses climbed up the mountain, the mountain of God, and out of a burning bush God spoke to him.

The fire had been there for a while, but it wasn't until Moses went to it that God was able to speak to him. Exodus 3:4 says that *"when the LORD saw that he* [Moses] *turned aside to look, God called to him."* God didn't call until Moses turned himself to the fire. The fire—the answer—is going to be right there next to us, but we have to turn to it if we want to hear God speak.

A lot of people say, "Well, if God wants to get hold of me, He'll get hold of me." Of course God can do that, but the Bible also says that Jesus is already at the door knocking (see Revelation 3:20). Why not just answer? What are you waiting for? For Him to break in a window? Why would you want to wait for God to break in on you when you can simply turn to Him and He will speak to you?

What God spoke to Moses that day transformed his life—and his world. He went from a rejected, exiled murderer to a powerful, world-famous civil rights leader . . . from a man wandering in the wilderness to a man of purpose who changed the destiny of a

nation. Not only that, but Moses also became the model for aboli-
tionists and civil rights leaders throughout history, from William
Wilberforce and Frederick Douglass to Martin Luther King, Jr.,
Gandhi, and Nelson Mandela.

Elijah called God *"the God who answers by fire"* (1 Kings 18:24) and
in Acts chapter 2, the Holy Spirit settled onto the heads of those
praying as *"tongues, as of fire"* (Acts 2:3). After that experience, they
went out and miracles happened. When we experience the fire of
God, good things follow.

When we are in a cold and rainy environment, we have to develop
the sense to go where the fire is. It's not going to change the
weather, but it is going to change you. Every Sunday, churches in your
area build fires for people to come to and find rescue. Go! Seek! Sit
in His presence! When you are in a storm, don't abandon church,
don't abandon your small group, and don't abandon your relationships, because those are key to your survival. So many times we abandon the *more* God has given us.

It's Not About the Cause, But About the Cure

When you are going through it, you need somebody to show up and
encourage you. You may not need their advice, but you'll need their
companionship. I have friends who have lost their homes, their
businesses, and their standing in their communities. I see them
come into church and they look a bit wet, a bit cold, and they are
shivering because of their storm. I can almost see that little dark
cloud following them around.

And often times when I begin to encourage them, it encourages
me as well. My encouragement becomes a *more* moment for them.
I begin to talk about the hope and faith and perseverance found in

Jesus' presence. I see the fire start to burn in their eyes again. Truly, there is power when somebody comes to speak faith into your life.

There is freedom from stress and anxiety when we remember what God's Word says. Jesus said, *"For where two or three are gathered together in My name, I am there in the midst of them"* (Matthew 18:20). Solomon, the wisest man to ever live, besides Jesus, also wrote:

> A person standing alone can be attacked and defeated, but two can stand back-to-back and conquer. Three are even better, for a triple-braided cord is not easily broken.
>
> *Ecclesiastes 4:12* NLT

Storms hit all of our lives. Now, I am not predicting that a storm is coming and I am not watching for a storm on the horizon. Storms just come. When Katrina hit New Orleans, it wasn't because New Orleans was a sinful city—if that were the case, why didn't it hit Las Vegas instead?

When Katrina hit New Orleans, it wasn't because New Orleans was a sinful city—if that is the case, why didn't it hit Las Vegas instead?

When the tidal wave hit Japan in 2011, it wasn't because God doesn't like the Japanese people or that they had somehow brought the calamity upon themselves. When the airliners hit the World Trade Center and Pentagon on September 11, 2001, it wasn't because the victims deserved it any more than a child stepping on a land mine in Cambodia is being punished for something she did.

We live in a world where bad things happen to people whether they deserve it or not. We live in a world of *less*. Whatever the insurance companies might call these, they are not "acts of God." They are random occurrences that happen in a world corrupted by sin, and that corruption does have repercussions, but not because some people deserve it more than others. God is not the cause, but He is the cure.

In the book of John, Jesus is asked an insightful question. When He and His disciples come across a man who was born blind, the disciples ask Jesus, "*Rabbi, who sinned, this man or his parents, that he was born blind?*" (John 9:2). Jesus' answer is, in a nutshell, "*Neither*" (John 9:3), "but," as I might paraphrase it, "as long as we are here, we might as well heal him."

Jesus wasn't looking for whom to blame, but instead wanted to see that "*the works of God should be revealed in him* [the blind man]" (John 9:3). My paraphrase would be, "Neither of them sinned, but this happened so that the God of More can show up!"

God didn't cause the man to be born blind; it just happened. But when the man connected with Jesus, He was more than willing to heal him. What Jesus is saying here is that it isn't about the cause, it is about the cure.

God didn't cause any of the things that were happening to us any more than He was responsible for Lazarus dying. But whether or not Lazarus was brought back to life again, Mary and Martha were better off for having Jesus with them. Jesus was touched by both their grief *and* their faith.

More than being a God of solutions, He is a God of compassion. He cares enough to be with us in our tragedies and storms and to connect with us in both our lowest and highest moments. The solutions don't always come the way we want, and sometimes that leaves us with big "Why?" questions. But He always comes when we seek Him with our whole hearts.

It reminds me of the scene in the movie *Knight and Day*. June Havens (Cameron Diaz) has to decide whether or not she will go with Roy Miller (Tom Cruise) or try to make it on her own. Miller holds his hand up about head level and says, "With me," then lowers it down, "without me." He is saying, "If you are with me, your experience—and chances of getting through this—is up here. Without me, they are down here." In any situation, we are better off with God than trying to do things on our own.

As we sought God in our grief and challenges, it wasn't our circumstances that changed first, it was us. I don't buy the argument that "God allowed these things to happen so He could teach us something;" but I know He is not one to miss a teachable moment when it comes. It is not about the lesson, though, it is about the connection with Him. It is about what we will do and become when the vise of life tightens around us.

> **As we sought God in our grief and challenges, it wasn't our circumstances that changed first, it was us.**

Will we blame God? Will we try to justify what happens with our own logic and reason? Will we apply our own limited understanding of justice to the situation? Will we lapse into denial or avoidance by busying ourselves with other things?

Or will we squarely face what is troubling us, call out and question God about it, and stay in His presence long enough for His peace and grace to soak into us so we can press forward just one more day? Will we trust the great God we serve and believe His perspective is higher than ours and that He has *more* in store for our lives?

That is what Wendy and I found ourselves doing, and there were times when the grace we found was just enough to get us to the next morning. Thankfully, "*Great is his faithfulness; his mercies begin afresh each morning"* (Lamentations 3:23 NLT). Though we may have felt exhausted by day's end, every morning we woke up to a fresh dose of grace and peace as we continued to seek and serve Him. Because of this, our perspective changed. We consistently saw the small miracles that God was performing around us. We celebrated how He had preserved us through even the worst of what we faced.

At times, life will give you less. However, while there is one who comes *"to steal, and to kill, and to destroy,"* there is also Jesus who said, *"I have come that they may have life, and that they may have it more abundantly"* (John 10:10). I'm telling you from personal experience, this is a promise that will get you *through.* The God of More will continually give you more and more of His power to strengthen you.

You will keep in perfect peace all who trust in you, all whose thoughts are fixed on you! Trust in the LORD *always, for the* LORD GOD *is the eternal Rock.*

Isaiah 26:3-4 NLT

Six

Calm
Within
the Storm

Just six weeks after my father-in-law passed away, we received an urgent phone call . . .

"Benny, this is Mom—everything looks fine, but your dad has had a heart attack and he's going to have surgery. You'll probably want to come down to see him."

I hung up the phone in shock. My only prayer at this helpless moment was, "Lord, I can't lose my dad too!"

Wendy and I packed as quickly as we could and hit the road for the four-hour trip to Los Angeles. In those four hours more revelations came to us about my own father's precarious position. The surgeon determined that the heart attack was much worse than initially thought, and he would require a quadruple bypass. We arrived in time to hug him, pray with him, and have a few moments together as a family. He went into surgery early the next morning.

The surgery was anticipated to be six hours long, so when we hit the eight-hour mark, the atmosphere in the waiting room underwent a distinct change. Questions, concern, and worry. Why was it taking so long? The surgeon finally called the family together to talk to us. He methodically went over the procedure he had just performed. In my dazed state, I heard "nine-way bypass" . . . "lost him on the table" . . . "he's on a ventilator now" . . . "the next 24 hours are critical."

"You can see him, but don't speak—just look."

Numb. I felt completely numb as we entered ICU to see my father hooked up to a ventilator and surrounded by medical equipment. The realization hit me that I'd been here before; this is exactly the way my father-in-law looked just a month and a half ago. Overwhelmed by the strikingly similar conditions, Wendy left the room in tears. I prayed for strength, but most of all I prayed for mercy. "Spare my dad's life, Lord."

> **The realization hit me that this is exactly the way my father-in-law looked just a month and a half ago.**

Miraculously, my dad pulled through. Each day, he grew stronger and was filled with renewed life. Each day, the gnawing fear subsided as I believed he would recover and my kids would have at least one grandpa on earth to hug.

All things considered, this was the first big victory for us in a while. Truthfully, we had steeled our hearts for the worst. It reminded me of Mark 9:24, when the father of a possessed boy comes to Jesus and asks for the boy to be made well. The father says to Jesus, "I believe; help my unbelief!"

That story gives me hope. Even in my moments of doubt or discouragement, God isn't mad at me or unwilling to work on my behalf. Sometimes we say to the Lord, "I believe it in my heart, but my mind is raging right now."

The bottom line is, where else would we go? Who else has the words of life? Don't get caught up in a moment of disheartenment. God is big enough to handle our weaknesses. I saw His hand distinctly as my dad made a miraculous recovery. My dad may have had his physical heart worked on, but I had my spiritual heart worked on.

God began the process of bypassing the pain, hurt, and disillusionment of the past eighteen months and helping me regain effectiveness. I felt the life of God pumping through my heart. I finally felt able to believe again.

There's no challenge to getting tossed to and fro by the waves of life. It happens to everyone. You

You may get pushed around uncontrollably for a while, but you still have the ability to choose your attitude.

certainly don't have to go looking for it. But there is a challenge to how you come out of whatever storm you are facing. You may get pushed around uncontrollably for a while, but you still have the ability to choose your attitude in the midst of the worst of things. You still have a choice between clinging to God or running from Him—of searching out godly companionship or isolating yourself and trying to self-medicate with anything from drugs and alcohol to food and television.

"Peace, Be Still!"

A story in Mark 4:35-41 features Jesus and the disciples in the midst of a storm:

> On the same day, when evening had come, He said to them, "Let us cross over to the other side." Now when they had left the multitude, they took Him along in the boat as He was. And other little boats were also with Him. And a great windstorm arose, and the waves beat into the boat, so that it was already filling. But He was in the stern, asleep on a pillow. And they awoke Him and said to Him, "Teacher, do You not care that we are perishing?"
>
> Then He arose and rebuked the wind, and said to the sea, "Peace, be still!" And the wind ceased and there was a great calm. But He said to them, "Why are you so fearful? How is it that you have no faith?" And they feared exceedingly, and said to one another, "Who can this be, that even the wind and the sea obey Him!"

Jesus has been teaching the disciples about His kingdom, a place where things happen according to the rules of heaven, not the ways of the earth. He gives them the vision of living in the will and power of God and then says, "Now we need to cross over to the other side of this sea and tell others about the kingdom of God." Then He promptly falls asleep in the back of the boat.

Imagine the disciples' excitement as they push off from the shore and into the open water, with His words still burning in their hearts. They must have been wondering, *What is going to happen next? Can you believe we are traveling with Jesus? This is amazing! Will things ever get any better than this?*

And then, right in the middle of their trip, a storm descends. With their heads filled with visions of heaven, they act as though they have never seen a storm before in their lives. They panic. Jesus, asleep, isn't worried about the storm. He didn't say, "Let's get in this boat to go to the other side—but of course, halfway through we will hit a storm." He left that last part out. He was so unconcerned about the storm that He took a nap.

Jesus said they were going to the other side. He said, "Let us cross over to the other side." In this sentence, "us" speaks of a relationship. It's "us"—you, me and Jesus—getting into the boat and going where He has directed. We are going where He has directed us to go and doing what He has directed us to do. It is not "me," nor is it "you"—it is "us." He is taking you to the other side. You are on your way. Just because you hit a storm or a roadblock doesn't mean you're not in the will of God.

> **Just because you hit a storm or a roadblock doesn't mean you're not in the will of God.**

Romans 8:6 tells us: "*letting the Spirit control your mind leads to life and peace*" (NLT). At the same time, Colossians 3:15 says, "*let the peace that comes from Christ rule in your hearts*" (NLT). The word "rule" in that verse can also be translated, "be an umpire . . . to decide, determine . . . to direct, control."[2] Furthermore, Paul told the Philippian believers:

> Be anxious for nothing, but in everything by prayer and supplication, with thanksgiving, let your requests be made known to God; and the peace of God, which surpasses all understanding, will guard your hearts and minds through Christ Jesus.
>
> *Philippians 4:6-7*

Regardless of the circumstances in the atmosphere around us, if we truly trust God in this way, His peace will lead us in every decision, even if that means we must "wait and see." We may not be called to sleep in the back of the boat, but there should be a sense of resting in God, even while the storms of life rage around us.

There is an eye in the middle of the hurricane where God keeps and protects our hearts. Paul says that peace may not even make any reasonable sense, but it is there, evermore present as we pursue Jesus more (see Philippians 4:7).

Jesus wants to be in relationship with you, and He wants you to be in relationship with Him. It is a partnership. That is the "Why?" of the cross—to be in relationship with us. The grace provided by Jesus pays the debt that separates each individual from God. It is how He equips and empowers us. It is the basis of our partnership with Him.

That doesn't mean there won't be times when you *feel* like God isn't right beside you. There are times it will seem like He is asleep in the back of the boat because you don't *feel* that He's with you. We have to determine which we trust more, His word or our feelings.

There will be times when you question if He is really with you or not—even if He really exists or not—just like the disciples questioned His word that they would make it to the other side. But when things get tumultuous, we can't forget He has promised to be with us. We have to remember the last thing He told us to do and hang on to that with both hands.

Maybe you say that He has never spoken to you. You know what I tell people who tell me that? I take my Bible, and I put it in front of my mouth like a duck's bill, and I open and close it like it's talking. I say, "This is my Word. This is me speaking to you."

God may never have spoken to you audibly. He may never have revealed something in your heart. You may not be able to tell the difference between His thoughts in your head and your own. But no matter what, we have the words He has written down for us in the Bible. He said, "*I will never leave you nor forsake you*" (Hebrews 13:5).

He didn't say, "You will always feel me with you," but He promised to be with us whether we feel His presence or not.

A Practical Love

If we are going to be in relationship with Jesus, we need to trust His Word and do as He directs. As He told His disciples, *"You are My friends if you do whatever I command you"* (John 15:14). He's not being legalistic and authoritarian when He says that; He is empowering us. Why? Because many of the things He tells us to do we can never do by ourselves. We can only truly do them when He empowers us to do them. That's why He sent the Holy Spirit to live in us and be with us at all times. He is with us to provide the ability to do what Jesus has called us to do. He is giving us the *more* to our *less*.

What do I mean? For me, it is virtually impossible to love my enemies. It is only by the power of God working in my heart that I don't try to get even when someone cuts me off on the freeway. I need the Holy Spirit to keep me focused on Jesus through all of life's ups and downs. Those things just aren't natural—that is why we need to tap into the supernatural.

Self-control is an outgrowth of being in relationship with God, as in a supernatural love that puts others before ourselves no matter what. And I am not talking about some kind of pie-in-the-sky concept of love that makes us feel better. I am talking about an actual, practical love that changes things when we act according to it.

> **It is only by the power of God that I don't try to get even when someone cuts me off on the freeway.**

That means we can't look at the Bible as a buffet. "I like this, but I don't like that. I am going to take this, but I am leaving all of that. I can love those who love me, but surely I can't love those who are a constant pain in the neck." If you are going to be a Christ-follower, you can't just pick what you want and ignore the rest.

> **When we set out onto the water with Jesus, there is no room for groupthink.**

When we set out onto the water with Jesus, there is no room for groupthink. Jesus never said, "Well, you guys get together and see what you can come up with and then get back to me." No! He wants us to walk in unity and brotherly love, but that only happens when each of us are on the same page with Jesus. Only then are we truly unified.

If you are in the boat with Jesus, you have to decide if you are just along for the ride or prepared to go wherever He wants to take you. Those just along for the ride shudder, murmur, and complain when the seas get rough. They are looking for the easy life, not the adventure of following Jesus. They are looking for a comfortable place to get by, not the turmoil of an emergency room trying to save people from the ambushes and calamities of this world. There are going to be some rough spots if we live for more than just ourselves.

That was Paul's example. He wasn't just trying to survive this world—he wanted desperately to change it. He wanted to influence others for righteousness . . . which is precisely the attitude that ushers into our lives the God of More.

I will sing to the LORD, *for He has triumphed gloriously . . . the* LORD *is my strength and my song; He has given me victory. This is my God and I will praise Him—my father's God, and I will exalt Him!*

Exodus 15:1-2 NLT

Seven

Feeding the Fire

Paul has just escaped death. He's narrowly avoided being thrown overboard and now he has endured a shipwreck. He lands on the island of Malta. He's cold, wet, and exhausted, and he's still being rained upon. You would think that he'd run to the fire to start drying out and warming up, but the Bible tells us he did something else instead. Paul starts picking up sticks to feed the fire. He makes a distinct choice.

> **Sometimes we think grace is the "pixie dust" sprinkled in the "Disney movie" of a Christian life.**

We make choices every day, whether it be in regard to our actions, thoughts, responses, or decisions. Daily, we hold the power of choice in our hands. I have a preschool-aged son, and I strive to teach him an important principle by teaching him a saying: "Grace is the power to choose to obey." Sometimes we think grace is the "pixie dust" sprinkled in the "Disney movie" of a Christian life.

My intent is not to discount grace, but instead to challenge the thought that just because I have God's favor on my life, nothing bad or demanding will ever happen to me. His grace makes a way, His grace is the way, and His grace is the power to complete the race set before us.

Paul made a choice to pick up sticks to fuel the fire. Fire is representative of God's presence. Sure, Paul could have just stumbled up the beach and run to the fire. Who would have blamed him after all he had been through? But he didn't.

Why is this so significant? Why would God put this small detail in this larger-than-life story? He wanted to give us another striking example of grace. Grace was not only the favor that protected Paul along his journey, but grace is the power to choose to fuel the fire even when still in the midst of the storm. In our own lives, oftentimes when we go through a storm of challenges, the last thing we want to do is attend to the small activities that nourish the presence of God—the fire of God, if you will—in our lives.

While it's important to get into the fire of God's presence, it's quite another thing to feed it so that its warmth increases in every area of our lives. We have to, by the grace of

> **While it's important to get into the fire of God's presence, it's quite another thing to feed it so that its warmth increases.**

God, pick up sticks to fuel the fire. That means we need to do things to continually feed God's presence in our lives.

It's the little things—sticking to the habits of seeking God. It's staying faithful in the things that help us grow: prayer, reading the

Bible, going to church, worship, giving. It's a matter of daily choosing peace, joy, hope, and love.

Generally, I get a mixed response when I say this. People ask me if I'm telling them to be fake, but I'm not asking you to fake it. Like my father-in-law used to say, "Faith it, don't fake it." The Bible says to walk by faith and not by sight. Walk by the promise of God, not by what you see naturally.

Choosing Joy

My father-in-law was such a great example of living by faith and by God's promises, and never living in denial. I used to think people were self-deceived when they chose joy, peace, love, prayer, and worship, as storms of adversity swirled around them.

I thought they were living in a fantasy, or they were just eternal optimists. But reading about Paul, I realized that choosing joy, service, and faith—even in the midst of a trial—isn't self-deception. It is truly choosing a Christ-centered outlook.

> **Regardless of your circumstances, you deserve the presence of God in your heart and life.**

It's believing what Jesus says about any and every situation. As Romans 8:37 says, *"In all these things we are more than conquerors through Him who loved us."* We don't usually see ourselves as more than conquerors, that is the part we have to take by faith—and the only way to lay hold of it is by faith.

Regardless of your circumstances, you deserve the presence of God in your heart and life. You deserve the love of God flooding your soul as you dive into the Bible. You deserve the peace that guards your heart diligently as you find your way into weekly fellowship with other believers in church. No matter what you are going through or how alone you feel, God is right there with you, ready to fulfill His promises.

I'm not asking you to pull out your happy face and put it on like a mask. I'm not saying to walk around pretending everything is okay. What I am saying is that you have a choice: be miserable in your storm or choose to fuel the fire in spite of your shipwreck. It might not change the situation, but it will certainly change your attitude.

Recently, I watched the Olympics and some gold-medal-winning athletes were being interviewed about the stress of competition and how they handled the immense pressure. Their responses were profound. Together they all agreed that they had repeated their routine thousands upon thousands of times, so when they got under the crushing pressure of the largest international sporting competition in the world, they said their bodies just took over and they performed from muscle memory. Their bodies just knew what to do because of what they had practiced many times before.

When you are going through a storm, there is a crushing pressure to let go, give up, crawl in bed, and pull the covers over your head. In moments of life when the waves are raging and emotional darkness is closing in, we need to have our diligent, daily "training" already in place. God is our lifeline, and we take hold of Him through the everyday spiritual disciplines. He is our strong tower. He is our *more*.

Paul knew this. He recognized the fire and in looking at it knew he needed to add to the blaze, continuing to do the little things to feed the fire of God in his life. For him it meant picking up sticks and throwing them onto the fire, even when he was tired, cold, and wet.

When do we need to do that? All of the time. We need to do it when it is sunny and warm, but we need to do it all the more when it is cold and rainy. When Wendy and I were really going through it, I had to keep going to church and preaching about God's hope and grace, even if I was preaching more to myself than anyone else.

Imagine that—a preacher who didn't want to go to church. Wendy had to keep leading worship. We kept faithful in choosing to feed the fire of God's presence in our lives, and it made all the difference in the world.

Somewhere between getting out of my bed and the end of the sermon, everything would change. I remember declaring God's Word in a sermon and feeling my own mind contradicting what I was saying. I might have been preaching "Jesus is the healer," and hearing my own thoughts asking, *Then why did your father-in-law die?*

> **I had to keep going to church and preaching about God's hope and grace, even if I was preaching more to myself than anyone else.**

Somewhere along the line as I continued to walk by faith, to speak God's Word and teach His truth, to minister even when I was heartbroken, somewhere in there things changed. As Paul told Timothy, *"Stir up the gift of God which is in you . . . For God has not given us a spirit of fear, but of power and of love and of a sound mind"* (2 Timothy 1:6-7).

It's only natural—especially if we are leaders of any kind—not to admit when we are in pain. We want to be positive, assure others we are doing well, and come across as if we have it all together. We want to talk about our victories and successes. That's not always a bad thing, but we have to be real as well.

There are times when it's more like, "God, I really don't want to be here. You know that. I'm just here because of You. I'm here because I want to be closer to You. You and me—we're going to make it through. We're going to go on and do this, no matter what." The grace to choose is there. Somewhere along the road of my tragedy, the questions stopped, the peace of God flooded my soul, and I knew God was going to see me through. My circumstances didn't change, God didn't change, but I changed.

Choose Your Church Boat

If we are going to cross to the other side of the sea in the midst of a storm, we have to get into the boat with Jesus. A boat is a vessel that gives you the ability to do something you would not otherwise be able to do. We go fishing in boats. We go waterskiing behind speedboats. Usually the fastest way we can travel from one side of a lake to the other is in a boat.

> **If we are going to get to the other side of the sea, we have to get in the boat with Jesus.**

To me, in the story of Jesus calming the storm, the boat represents the local church (see Mark 4). The church gives us the ability to do something we would not otherwise be able to do. The church is unique in its purpose. It is the mission of the local church to help people grow and be transformed into the likeness of Jesus.

The local church is the place of accountability. The local church is the place where God works on our character. The local church is the place where our gifts, talents, and abilities are discovered, honed, and released. The local church is the place where we learn to serve in God's house. The local church is where you bring your tithes and offerings so we can do more things for the glory of God. The local church was never man's idea; it was God's idea.

Certainly, the local church has different expressions, traditions, and practices. That's why there are Baptists, Presbyterians, Lutherans, non-denominational believers, and many others. There are different expressions for different personalities within the body. But the local church is the place where being a Christian really happens. It is the only way to get into the boat with Jesus. As Rick Warren once tweeted, "There is no such thing as a Christian living outside of community," and that community is first and foremost the local church.

People ask me, "Which church should I be in?" The answer: a church you will faithfully attend and a church that has Jesus at the center.

> "Which church should I be in?" The answer: a church you will faithfully attend and a church that has Jesus at the center.

a church that has Jesus at the center. Do not go to a church that is exalting something or someone else. The right church for you will be one that preaches Jesus, loves Jesus, worships Jesus, and serves and loves its community like Jesus. It doesn't have to be big; it just has to have Jesus at the center.

Do you think Jesus knew there was going to be a storm halfway across the sea when He told His disciples to get into the boat (see Mark 4:35)? Sure, He did. Do you think He knew how bad it was going to be? Of course He did. So what did He do? He went to sleep. Why would God fall asleep in the middle of your storm? Because God is more certain of the spiritual reality of His Word than the temporary reality of our storms.

Jesus said, "Let's go to the other side." That was good enough for Him. The winds weren't in charge; the Creator of the winds was. But the disciples saw the storm with all its danger. They had been fishermen all their lives and knew the perils of going out in the waters when there was a storm. So they woke Jesus and told Him, "We're going to die! Don't you even care, Jesus? We're not going to make it!"

How many of us have been guilty of the exact same thing—telling God the final outcome, as if we know better than He does? We have to quit telling God the end of our story. We think, *Maybe God doesn't know what is going to happen? Maybe He's asleep, and I better wake Him up and tell Him what is going to happen!*

There's only one person who knows the end from the beginning—there's only one person that knows tomorrow—and His name is Jesus. We need to calm down and quit telling God what the end result will be. We need to ask Him instead, because He already has it all figured out. We need to learn to rest in His grace and peace. We need to trust that He has the situation well in hand.

> **We need to calm down and quit telling God what the end result will be.**

When storms hit, many people want to quit. They say, "Hey, I didn't sign up for this! I don't have to take this! I'm out of here!" They quit their job, they give up on their marriage, leave their family, resign from their church, or abandon their faith. I understand that feeling; I can relate. Please see these words as hope.

Find yourself a good Bible translation that is easy to understand, invest in some good worship CDs or downloads. Find a church where you can be planted. No church is perfect, but you need community. Paul went to a fire that someone else had built for him. I know what that is like.

There Is No Plan B

At the end of the day, this isn't just something I do; this is something I have been *called* to do. I have no option "B"! God saved me, He changed me, He has shown me His goodness and grace and what it can do. I don't even want to think about where I'd be if it weren't for Him.

When things aren't going so well, do you stop to think about what God has already done for you? If all He had ever done was save me—if all He had ever done was give me eternal life—that's already *more* than I could ever have expected or deserved. But that's not all God does. He is so good in the midst of your storms: He still blesses, He still makes things right, He still provides. But sometimes we have to persevere through tough places as we see those blessings come to pass.

> I have no option "B"! God saved me, He changed me, He has shown me His goodness and grace and what it can do.

I've learned that when things are bad, I can't just sit and hope things will get better. I have to pick up the "sticks" of Bible reading, praying, and choosing a good attitude. I have to pick up the sticks of friendship and encouragement. I have to call my friend Pastor Chris in Denver and say, "Chris, I need you to pray with me."

I have to feed the fire of God in my life because I know there is no other source of help and comfort that will make a difference in any situation. Only He can give me the grace, the power, to continue.

What do you need to do today to fuel His presence in your life? Obey? Pray? Love? Have a good attitude? Go to church? Pick up

those sticks, make a grace-filled choice today in spite of your circumstances. As Scripture says:

> For I know the thoughts that I think toward you, says the LORD,
> thoughts of peace and not of evil, to give you a future and a hope.
>
> *Jeremiah 29:11*

I know it's not easy to fuel the fire of God in your life when you're
soaked to the bone by life's storms. But Wendy and I are living
examples. We did it, and so can you.

"I have given you authority over all the power of the enemy, and you can walk among snakes and scorpions and crush them. Nothing will injure you."

Luke 10:19 NLT

Eight

Snake Bit!

Shortly after Easter of 2011, negotiations with the bank regarding our church's mortgage and greatly depreciated property came to a halt. Due to circumstances beyond our control, the only way forward was to begin the process of filing chapter 11 bankruptcy as a church. This was one of the single most crushing days of my life. I have never felt so defeated.

Personally, Wendy and I could have walked away from the church building and been fine. The clincher, though, was that we wouldn't have been just walking away from a building and property—after all, the church is not just a building with furniture and equipment. The church is people. It's all about people.

There were staff and church members who were giving their all to reach Las Vegas, as well as thousands who found each weekend worship experience a lifeline. We were pastors and this was our family. We couldn't walk out on them or on Las Vegas. Bottom line: we were called.

Once we filed for bankruptcy, criticism came from many different vantage points. This all hurt more than you would think. With my background in accounting, finances have always been strong for the church and for our family.

I take financial responsibility very seriously. We made a point of doing everything above board and according to the strictest principles of financial trusteeship. Of all the places in which we thought we had been conscientious, we considered financial integrity to be the last area where we would get criticized.

Picking Up Sticks on a Rainy Day

Paul, a great man of faith if ever there was one, got caught in the same storm as unbelievers. He was grounded on the same sandbar, saw his ship get torn to pieces just as they did, swam for shore and floated on the same pieces of the ship, alongside his shipmates. They saw the same fire. When Paul decided to pick up sticks to feed the fire, things only got worse. As Paul began to feed the fire, a viper fastened itself onto Paul's hand. Suddenly, things were far worse for him than anyone else.

In Acts 28:3, we read how the heat of the fire drove out the viper. The snake bit the hand that was feeding the fire. In classical literature and mythology, snakes have long represented evil forces. Time and again in the book of Acts, when Paul went to a new city to free the people from the oppression of the religious temples and idol makers, he and his companions met opposition. The gospel has a strange way of upsetting power structures, especially those structures that depend on manipulating other people for control and profit.

In Philippi (whose ruins can be found in northern Greece today), one man was using his slave girl as a fortuneteller. When she came to Paul and was delivered from the spirit of divination that possessed her, her master became infuriated. He had Paul and his associate, Silas, thrown into prison (see Acts 16:16-24).

In Derbe, Paul so upset the local religious power structure that they pummeled him with stones and left him for dead (see Acts 14:19-20). In Ephesus, a local silversmith, who made most of his money by creating statues of the local favorite goddess, Diana, was so incensed that he organized a riot with the other merchants and had Paul dragged before the authorities (see Acts 19:21-41). In Thessalonica, Paul and his companions were accused of turning "*the world upside down*" (Acts 17:6).

After all these hardships and more, Paul found himself with a snake's jaws clamped down on his hand. Snakes usually only attack when they feel threatened, or to protect their territory. That certainly seems to fit Paul's experience, with the literal snake and the "snakes" he encountered during his ministry endeavors. Every time he came into a city and threatened to upset the power brokers or to free people from spiritual or physical bondage, the snakes came out to attack.

In the late 1800s, when drinking was such a problem in English towns that it destroyed families and kept a significant percentage of the population unemployed, local tavern owners and distillers organized a "Skeleton Army" to march into the streets and oppose the charitable work of the Salvation Army, which was delivering people from the power alcohol had over them.

This Skeleton Army was made up of thugs and bullies who threw rotten fruit and vegetables at Salvation Army bands and speakers, who were sometimes even beaten simply for telling people about the healing power of Jesus. In response, the charitable workers wore their bruises and cuts, bandages and slings, like medals of honor.

When Snakes Bite

When you start to do good in an area and disrupt power or profit, it isn't unusual that you will force snakes out of their holes. When the message of freedom in Jesus Christ starts to take hold in an area, snakes will bite. For example, the efforts our church has made to end sex trafficking has upset "serpents" in the Las Vegas valley.

> **When the message of freedom in Jesus Christ starts to take hold in an area, snakes will bite.**

A lot of people think that legalizing and regulating prostitution decreases illegal prostitution in the area, but it actually increases it. While prostitution is not legal in Clark County, whose county seat is Las Vegas, it is legal in brothels in the next county to the northwest, Nye County. This has caused an increased market for prostitution in Las Vegas.

Research shows that wherever prostitution has been legalized around the world, there will be an increase in the pedaling of under-aged girls, many of whom are runaways or orphans. They become easy targets because no one is around to speak up for them. This market is so great that traffickers will ship girls in from other nations halfway around the world to pedal them on the streets of Las Vegas.

Girls from Eastern Europe and Asia are common. Human trafficking is the most profitable and insidious form of black market trading the world knows. If you traffic guns or drugs, you can sell them once, but if you traffic children and women, you can sell them several times a day.

Trafficking children into prostitution will become a peripheral industry wherever prostitution has been legalized. Both Germany and the Netherlands are already considering repealing their legalization of prostitution because of the problems it has caused, and Sweden has gone so far as to say that allowing a woman to be exploited as a prostitute is a human rights violation. Being a prostitute is both demeaning and dangerous.

The mortality rate for those in prostitution is forty times (not 40 percent, but forty times!) higher than it is for any other occupation. Women involved in prostitution are routinely threatened, beaten, and far too often, murdered.

And that is not even mentioning the dangers of STDs, AIDS, and other health issues they face. Most people don't concern themselves about it because they think these women have chosen this lifestyle for themselves, but even those who do are being duped about what prostitution really does to them.

Women and girls—and even young boys—who get into prostitution rarely do it as anything other than a last resort, if they are doing it willingly at all. Studies show that four out of five of the women in legal brothels in Nevada urgently want out as well. You can only imagine how much higher that desire is among women in illegal prostitution. The statistics are one thing, but to hear the stories of the women and girls who have come through our church is heartbreaking.

Just because you were bitten by snakes doesn't mean that you are doing something wrong—in fact, it probably means you are doing something right. When you stir up the fire of God in your life, there are going to be some snakes to deal

> **The enemy will always bite the hand that is feeding the fire.**

with. There are going to be issues or accusations that are aimed at making you feel discouraged, guilty, condemned, and alone.

The enemy will always bite the hand that is feeding the fire. When a church advocates for its city and starts being generous, enemy forces will strike at it. There is a constant spiritual battle taking place between the forces of good and evil, light and darkness, righteousness and sinfulness.

If you get bit by a snake, that's not the time for an internet study into the nature of snakes and how lethal their venom might potentially be. Once bit, what's your natural response? You withdraw your hand and shout, "Ouch!" Your reaction is not to calmly study what just happened, but to withdraw your hand as quickly as possible.

When the enemy bites you, it is because he wants you to withdraw the hand that has been feeding the fire of God's presence in your life. I know the feeling: When Wendy and I got "bit" by one tough situation after another, I felt like withdrawing my hand. I wanted to pull back from what we were doing in Las Vegas that made us a flashpoint for controversy. I wanted to pull back on giving because maybe we wouldn't have enough.

Look at what happened to the apostle Paul. He's feeding the fire, the fire drives out a viper, and the viper latches onto his hand. He's standing there looking at the snake, the people all around are looking at the snake, and what is their first thought? *"No doubt this man is a murderer, whom, though he has escaped the sea, yet justice does not allow to live"* (Acts 28:4). Their first response is, "He must've done something wrong to deserve what happened to him!" Not only does Paul get bit by a snake, but he also gets bit by criticism and condemnation.

It's Not Us Versus Them

What's our first thought when we see someone walking through a storm? Certainly, there are times when people are in unfortunate circumstances because of something they have done, but here's what Jesus tells us: *"Do not judge others, and you will not be judged"* (Matthew 7:1 NLT). He didn't say, "Analyze the lives of others so you can figure out where they went wrong."

No, He says, *"How can you think of saying to your friend, 'Let me help you get rid of that speck in your eye,' when you can't see past the log in your own eye?"* (Matthew 7:4 NLT). In essence He is saying, "Don't forget, when you point a finger at someone else, there are three fingers pointing back at you!" As Jesus points out, deliverance from the logs in our own eyes comes only when we are more interested in helping others than judging them.

> **If we want to be more like Jesus, then our response should not be in blaming, but in comforting and healing.**

Many times it's nothing you did, it's just a storm you're going through. Sometimes there's no secret sin, there's no big mistake —it's just life. If we want to be more like Jesus, then our response should not be in blaming and telling others they messed up, but in comforting and healing.

Our most fulfilling life will not be based on criticisms, but encouragement. Our calling as people of faith is to help others get through their storms and arrive at a safe harbor. The grace of God is based on no condemnation, no untouchables, no "us" versus "them." The phrase that ought to guide us all: "There, but for the grace of God, go I."

The same sins Jesus paid for you, He also paid for others. The same gap between you and God that Jesus closed, He also closed for others—all we have to do is accept and believe what He did and then start acting according to it. The grace of God is available to make up the difference for everyone who will accept it. This is the true definition of *more*.

In the 1800s, the slave trade out of Africa was the most brutal and calloused the world had ever known. Men, women, and children were beaten mercilessly for the slightest infraction of a ship's rules—declared in the captives' own language. If a slave was ill, that individual and anyone he or she was chained to would get thrown overboard to keep the disease from spreading.

It wasn't uncommon for ships to arrive with half the number of slaves they had captured. Those below deck were stacked like books on shelves into claustrophobic spaces, shoulder-to-shoulder with people they had never met before. Families were ripped apart. The captains of these ships were brutal men with virtually no regard for the value of life.

Yet one such man, named John Newton, recognized the inhumanity of his trade and called out to Jesus for forgiveness. By all that is just, if God was to turn anyone away from heaven, it would be a man like John Newton. But God didn't. For the lashings John had ordered onto the backs of African slaves, Jesus had taken lashings to pay for John's sins.

That is grace. John was so moved by what he experienced that he put words to a tune he had heard. In doing so, he penned what is arguably the greatest Christian song of all time, "Amazing Grace." The music is in the pentatonic scale of West Africa and likely a tune John had heard rising out of the belly of his ship as the captives below mourned their homes. Out of their pain emerged a song of grace that has been repeated in nearly every Christian church since.

That is grace—something that comes out of sin and loss, something that creates beauty where there was pain and suffering before, something that closes up the divide between a brutal mass murderer, a child molester or rapist, a thief and a traitor, a prostitute and a pimp, and God in heaven. For where there is lack and bondage because of sin, God has supplied more grace to make up the difference between what you deserve and who God dreamed you could become.

I don't know what pain or sense of worthlessness or feelings of being "less than" you may have experienced in your life, but that is not from God. What *is* from God is the more that comes through grace. As we experienced some of the suffering that comes with loss and criticism, we also began to understand why it is said God's peace *"exceeds anything* [you] *can understand"* (Philippians 4:7 NLT).

I don't know what feelings of being "less than" you may have experienced, but that is not from God.

It makes no sense to have the world falling down around you and have perfect peace at the same time, but we began to experience a glimpse of that peace—that sense of *more*. That doesn't mean we didn't hurt, didn't doubt ourselves, didn't want to lash out at those who said bad things about us, but it did mean there were times we felt God with us and we knew we were going to get through.

I cried out, "I am slipping!" but Your unfailing love, O LORD, supported me. When doubts filled my mind, Your comfort gave me renewed hope and cheer.

Psalm 94:18-19 NLT

Nine

Shake It Off!

As we were enduring our storms, so were many of our church friends. Mark and Tina, whose family had been part of our church from the beginning, were a prime example. I remember sitting with Mark in my office, looking at each other with tears in our eyes, sharing what was happening in our lives, and having no idea what to do with our "Why?" questions.

Mark and Tina had been faithful givers to the church since the beginning, and with the economic downturn, jobs for his subcontracting business were drying up, revenues were down 60 percent, he was a quarter of a million dollars upside-down in his family home, and his savings were all but depleted.

In the years of the boom, his business had thrived. A few years before the bust, he had invested in a building, and now between salaries, mortgage, and other expenses, he had no idea how he was going to make ends meet moving forward.

So we put our heads together and prayed. When we looked up at each other after saying "Amen," it wasn't as if we received complete peace about the situation or a revelation about the future. In many ways, nothing had really changed, except that now we had more of a commitment to move forward *together*, trusting God, and relying on His grace more than our own wisdom and understanding.

It also helped us that Mark's life verse is Proverbs 3:5-6:

> Trust in the LORD with all your heart,
>   And lean not on your own understanding;
> In all your ways acknowledge Him,
>   And He shall direct your paths.

Things didn't immediately get better. There were definitely some blows to Mark's ego along the way. As a respected man of God in the church who had always been seen as a wise leader, it was humbling to make tough financial decisions. As the provider for one's family, it's extremely tough to explain to people—who have viewed you as "blessed by God"—that you are losing your home.

How do you find words to tell them that you are going to have to "short sell" it because you can't make the mortgage payments? How do you tell them you are going to move in with your in-laws to make it through? I really felt for what Mark and his family were experiencing.

But Mark and Tina stayed faithful in the church. We met and prayed several times, and they handled one decision at a time. They sold their house for nearly a quarter million less than what their mortgage had been, and the bank forgave the money they lost on the home. They moved into Tina's parents' home, which happened to be large enough that they weren't tripping over each other. Mark went to work each morning, picked up the sticks of daily devotions, and kept trusting God. If Mark gained anything in this season, it was a passion for God like never before—not just a *sustaining* passion, but an *advancing* one.

Real Friends and a Real God

When someone walks through a storm like this, that person doesn't need answers from a finite mind that tries to determine cause and effect. It is easy to blame or find fault, but that is rarely helpful. It would be easy to say Mark had missed God in some major way or else he wouldn't have been in his desperate situation. But that wouldn't have helped him move forward.

> **If Mark gained anything it was a passion for God like never before—not just a *sustaining* passion, but an *advancing* one.**

What Mark needed was a friend who continued to point toward God, who mourned and prayed together with him in brotherly love, who was there to support him through the storm. He needed to know there were people who would stick with him no matter what. How do I know? Because these were the things I needed as we faced our own storm, and Mark was that kind of friend to me.

So Mark and Tina disregarded the obstacles and moved forward following God's leading. Things didn't get better all through 2010 and 2011, but somehow they didn't get worse either. Looking back now, and reviewing his financial books from 2011, Mark still doesn't understand how he kept salaries, mortgage, and monthly expenses paid.

He even had money left over to feed his family, as well as continue to give to the church. It made no logical sense. The numbers just didn't seem to add up, but somehow, even with less coming in each month, he never stopped tithing or taking care of his family's needs.

Then he learned that the downturn had also hit his father-in-law hard (who worked for a general contractor), and had it not been for the rent money they paid them, his in-laws might have lost their home as well. Somehow there was sufficient grace to make it through each day, and as that happened day after day, there was sufficient grace for each week and month that led to making it through the year.

In the last quarter of 2011, a non-Christian man came to Mark on referral and offered some work. Usually, Mark worked only with contractors he knew, but he sensed this was a divine appointment. The result was that in the last three months of 2011, Mark's business brought in more than it had the entire previous year.

Not only that, but as Mark walked humbly through his trials, the man watched him and started asking him questions about his faith. Mark found he had a new avenue to talk about Jesus with people he worked with, and this man would be only the first. As Mark put it, what he went through "promoted a lot of thought and a lot of questions in people we may not have been able to reach unless we had gone through some of these storms."

About nine months after their short sale, Mark and Tina learned about a mortgage program that was only for people who had not filed bankruptcy or had a short sale in the previous two years. Despite the fact that they didn't qualify, Mark and Tina felt led to investigate it.

As a result, even before the two-year period passed, Mark and Tina were able to move their family into a renovated, gorgeous new home that was larger than the one they had lost. Because they had been frugal and faithful to save while in Tina's parents' home, they were able to make a substantial down payment on the home, reduce their interest rate to 1.875 percent, and miraculously move in with a good bit of equity already in the house.

As the end of the school year approached in the spring of 2012, Mark's business was again on track to meet all of its projections, they enjoyed their new home, and they had a sense of stability for the first time in a long time. You can hardly talk to Mark or Tina today and not have them rave about what Jesus brought them through. Their life exemplifies how God gives more when life gives you less.

Mark and Tina are not the same people they were before these storms. It is not that they are any more faith-filled or prosperous now than they were before. Nor are they suddenly remarkably better parents or spouses, though they do have newfound appreciation for balancing work and home.

Mark and Tina were both great people going into all of this, and they are still great people coming out . . . though they do carry themselves differently. Their trust in God is more seasoned. They are more transparent. They understand what it is like to be in the midst of a storm and what it takes to make it to the shore on the other side. Their empathy is more genuine; their advice is more grace-filled. They seem like people who can say somewhat what Paul said in Philippians:

> I know how to live on almost nothing or with everything. I have learned the secret of living in every situation, whether it is with a full stomach or empty, with plenty or little. For I can do everything through Christ, who gives me strength.
>
> *Philippians 4:12-13* NLT

God Is Not Worried About the Economy

Looking back on those years, I remember going to staff meetings and discussing all the numbers of what was coming in and what was going out and wondering how we were still making budget. I remember talking about all we were doing in the community and how tight it was as far as paying salaries or meeting our monthly expenses.

The experience of Mark and his family was far from unique among our members. I remember in the midst of those meetings having my mind scream that we should reduce our giving and generosity to the ministries and outreaches we were supporting.

We had to save money and keep more back as a reserve against the next storm that was likely to hit us. My mind was screaming, *Withdraw your hand of tithing! Withdraw your hand of offering! Withdraw your hand of supporting other ministries! We have to be ready for whatever hits us next!*

But at the same time, my spirit spoke to me: "Don't do that! If you give to the poor, you lend to the Lord and the Lord is a debtor to no man. God is not worried about the economy. Heaven hasn't lost any value. Are you going to be ruled by circumstances or what God promises to do in His Word?"

> God is pulling us back in a slingshot, because He is going to shoot us far into the future faster than we can imagine.

So I would look up at my staff—who had no idea of the war going on within me—and say, "Listen, we are not Christians who draw back when times get tough. We will not be intimidated by what the devil throws at us. We are not people who say, 'Oh, we've been attacked! We need to retreat!' No! There is no retreat! There is no backing up, backing down, or pulling back! What the enemy has meant for evil, God will turn to good. We are in God's hands, God is pulling us back in a slingshot, because He is going to shoot us far into the future faster than we can imagine. But we have to stay faithful to what He has called us to do. We can't look at the circumstances and be ruled by how much the wind howls. We have to look at God's Word and be ruled by what *it* says."

How could I say that? How could I ask my staff to take that course of action that puts even greater strain on limited resources? Because that is just what the apostle Paul did. When that snake bit him, he didn't withdraw his hand. He didn't stop feeding the fire. He didn't scream and run away in a panic.

He was standing there tossing sticks into the fire—a viper latches onto his hand and he lifts it up looking at it for a fraction of a second. So what does Paul do? Paul shakes the snake off into the fire. He's not even concerned. Then he goes back to doing what he had been doing before—feeding the fire.

Despite the fact that it was Paul who saved the crew through prayer, or that he was in the middle of the will of God, or that he was innocent of any crime, people still automatically assumed the worst. When they realized all that had happened to him and then saw a snake hanging from his hand, they decided he was, *"A murderer, no doubt! Though he escaped the sea, justice will not permit him to live"* (Acts 28:4 NLT). They were convinced he was guilty of something horrible and that justice was going to get him in the end, no matter what.

> **If you build your self-identity on what people think about you, you'll drive yourself crazy.**

Then, when he didn't swell up and die, people's perceptions changed to the other extreme: "He's not a murderer; he's a god!"

If you build your self-identity on what people think about you, you'll drive yourself crazy. "Oh, he's a murderer!" "Oh, he's a god!"

No, he's a man—a man who has given his life to Jesus and is on a mission to do what God called him to do. It is not our responsibility to win any popularity contests with people. It is only our responsibility to make sure we are obeying God the best we can. It is up to us to put Him first and live according to what He tells us we should do. This won't keep the storms away, but it is the best way to make it through them and come out stronger on the other side.

We need to realize that the grace of God is our greatest help in time of need. What Jesus paid for by shedding His blood on the cross and what God exercised in raising Jesus from the grave—these are not just the central tenets of our faith, they are the sole source of empowerment for the Christian life.

Grace is the doorway back to a relationship with God; it is the food that nurtures the fruit of the Spirit; it is the medium in which the gifts of the Spirit operate. It is the manna of our existence as Christ-followers.

Grace is so powerful that we even see it exemplified in the natural world. In the olden days, in order to make an antidote for snake venom, people would take the venom of the viper and mix it with the blood of a lamb. When they did this, the blood of the lamb would make antibodies that would overcome the venom's poison. It was an incredibly effective antivenom.

In the spiritual sense, more than 2,000 years ago there was a Lamb who was slain on a tree for you and me—and now, according to Revelation 12:11, we overcome the enemy by the blood of the

Lamb and the word of our testimony. The power of the blood is more potent than the venom of a viper.

We even see a foreshadowing of this in the Old Testament. While in the desert, the Israelites complained and murmured against God and Moses saying, *"Why have you brought us up out of Egypt to die in the wilderness? For there is no food and no water, and our soul loathes this worthless bread"* (Numbers 21:5). Similar to what happened to Paul, out of rocks, vipers came and began to bite the people. Seeing the error of their ways, the people repented and asked Moses to call upon God to forgive and heal them. When Moses prayed, God told him to *"make a fiery serpent, and set it on a pole; and it shall be that everyone who is bitten, when he looks at it, shall live"* (Numbers 21:8).

Now that seems a little crazy, doesn't it? Why didn't God just heal them? Because the act was symbolic of salvation itself. John 3:14-15 tells us, *"As Moses lifted up the serpent in the wilderness, even so must the Son of Man be lifted up, that whoever believes in Him should not perish but have eternal life."*

Those who lifted up their eyes and looked at the serpent on a pole that Moses fashioned out of bronze were saved; those who did not, died. It is the same instruction to us today: in our storms, we must lift up our eyes to Jesus.

Furthermore, Moses made the serpent out of bronze. Throughout the Bible, bronze is related to judgment. Altars were commonly made of acacia wood and overlaid with bronze. The utensils and grates for the altar were also made of bronze (see Exodus 27:1-4). As Philippians 2:5-8 tells us:

> Let this mind be in you which was also in Christ Jesus, who, being in the form of God, did not consider it robbery to be equal with God, but made Himself of no reputation, taking the form of a bondservant, and coming in the likeness of men. And being found

in appearance as a man, He humbled Himself and became obedient to the point of death, even the death of the cross.

Just as the bronze serpent was a likeness of sin and judgment, so Jesus was raised up for all to see on the cross *"in the likeness of sinful flesh"* (Romans 8:3), that sin might be condemned and *"that the righteous requirement of the law might be fulfilled in us who do not walk according to the flesh but according to the Spirit"* (Romans 8:4).

God's "More" May Not Be What We Expect

The judgment for all sin was paid for by the blood Jesus shed on the cross—in essence, the venom of sin was mixed with the blood of the Lamb. And though the sin that exists in the world might make us suffer for a time, it does not have the power to separate us from God if we lift up our eyes to Jesus—that the forgiveness and the grace of God might come upon us.

I also believe this is why Mark 16:17-18 tells us *"these signs will follow those who believe: . . . they will take up serpents; and if they drink anything deadly, it will by no means hurt them."* I don't think that means we should be handling snakes as part of our Sunday services, but that it is symbolic of what Paul did—he "picked up" the viper, looked at it for a moment, then shook it off into the fire. The poison had no effect on him because his eyes were firmly fixed on Jesus, the one who had saved him from the storm, the shipwreck, and the snake!

Paul didn't ask, "Oh, God, have I not served you faithfully? Don't I deserve better than this? Why was I in the storm? Why was I shipwrecked? Why did you allow me to be bitten by a deadly viper? Why is all of this happening to me?" No, Paul just shook off the snake and went back to feeding the fire. He didn't get sidetracked with worrying about the "Why?" questions. He was only interested in the cure, and Jesus is the antidote for every bite.

Trying to be comforting, people have told me things like, "Oh, God must have wanted your baby more." No way! I wanted my baby more. My father-in-law didn't suffer and die because of some secret will of God. Why did he die? Why didn't our faith see him cured by the grace of God? I don't know. But I do know he is happier now than he has ever been seeing his Savior face to face. His victory was not the victory we had asked for, but does that mean it was not a victory all the same? I still don't have all the answers to my "Why?" questions, but I am all the more determined to embrace the grace that is the power to see us through.

> **People have told me things like, "Oh, God must have wanted your baby more." No way! I wanted my baby more.**

We need to stop worrying about the causes so much and get caught up in the cure. When we get bitten by the "viper of sin" in this world, we don't need to stop there and write a theological doctoral dissertation on the snake that is hanging from our hand. What we need to do is shake it off. We need to shake off the viper by being generous and being a blessing to others no matter what is happening in our lives. The *more* of the blood of the Lamb is the ability to stand firm in spite of pain, to believe when it seems impossible, to give when it seems illogical, to love even when someone seems unlovable.

Through the storm, through crisis or calamity, Jesus has promised never to leave us or turn His back on us. Sometimes the *more* from God isn't always what we think it ought to be. The *more* isn't always the absence of problems or a magic wand that removes every obstacle. Sometimes *more* is tapping into a deeper grace and empowerment from the Lord than you ever knew was possible. Sometimes *more* is the ability to move on, without bitterness, even when the "Whys?" go unanswered.

Sometimes *the more* is trusting that God will "*work all these things out together for our good*" (see Romans 8:28), even when circumstances look hopeless. It doesn't matter if

> **The *more* of the blood of the Lamb is the ability to stand firm in spite of pain.**

we are facing our own faults, or just a matter of a storm front rolling through our lives. He is still there, knocking at the door, ready to come in and be with us if we would just open the door.

Paul's realization of this is what got him to his "Malta moment"—the moment in which, just as things got to their worst when that viper latched onto his hand, God turned the tables and changed what the enemy had meant for harm into something very good.

The LORD says, "I will rescue those who love Me. I will protect those who trust in My name. When they call on Me, I will answer; I will be with them in trouble. I will rescue and honor them. I will reward them with a long life and give them My salvation."
Psalm 91:14-16 NLT

Ten

The Malta Moment

Did Wendy and I get a Malta moment like Paul's? Was there a day in which everything changed, when the clouds seemed to part? Well, while the ultimate end of our story has yet to be written, 2012 brought incredible changes for us—changes that happened even in the midst of writing this book. Jesus does take storms and turn them into triumphs. Jesus does see you through. Jesus does give you *more*.

As we continued to walk through our church's chapter 11 bankruptcy and a stringent debt-reduction strategy, the bank suddenly approached us with a settlement. We had a miracle appear before our eyes . . . but without the needed finances to take advantage of the offer. We literally needed *another* financial miracle to make this negotiation miracle a possibility. It looked hopeless.

After coming so far, it seemed for a moment that we were done. I remember coming home to my wife and saying, "It's over. We've lost." The settlement opportunity seemed beyond our reach.

Then, the very next day, I received an international phone call from a businessman who had never even been to our church. Because we had a mutual friend, he'd heard about our need and wanted to help. He said he would talk with his wife and call me back. I really didn't know what to expect.

The next day I waited impatiently for his phone call. This gentleman told me he and his wife had agreed to loan us $2.3 million to close out the negotiations with our bank and, on top of that, they would give us another lump sum to help cover other costs in closing the deal. Only God can take a man we didn't even know and speak to him about a church in Las Vegas and convince him to help.

Suddenly, after what seemed like a storm that would never end, in a few months' time we were able to settle with the bank, end our pursuit of bankruptcy, clear our debt, and finally see the clouds begin to part and let the sunshine through again.

I remember thinking several times in the midst of the storms, *I must have been out of God's will when I bought the property*. But looking at it now, nothing could be further from the truth. How God worked this out was truly miraculous and very much the way He likes to do things—He did so much more than we could ask, think, or even imagine.

It seemed just like the Psalm says:

> I waited patiently for the LORD to help me,
>   and he turned to me and heard my cry.
> He lifted me out of the pit of despair,
>   out of the mud and the mire.
> He set my feet on solid ground
>   and steadied me as I walked along.
> He has given me a new song to sing,
>   a hymn of praise to our God.

Many will see what he has done and be amazed.

They will put their trust in the LORD.

Oh, the joys of those who trust the LORD,

who have no confidence in the proud

or in those who worship idols.

O LORD my God, you have performed many wonders for us.

Your plans for us are too numerous to list.

You have no equal.

If I tried to recite all your wonderful deeds,

I would never come to the end of them.

Psalm 40:1-5 NLT

Hello, Hurricane!

Paul's Malta moment didn't come without adventure. Arrested, imprisoned, deported, lost at sea, shipwrecked, and then snake bitten—Paul had been through the storm, but never lost his sense of balance because throughout it all, he remained firmly anchored to the Rock. If anything, his faith in the promises of God became stronger, not weaker. He'd been through the hurricane, but all it did was strip away every other concern about his life. With no possessions, no job, no home, and no family, Paul stood there by the fire, feeding sticks into it.

> **While the enemy had meant to destroy Paul, instead his faith was strengthened and his reputation was increased.**

While the enemy had meant to destroy Paul, instead his faith was strengthened and his reputation was increased among all who were with him, leading to the salvation of many. The book of Acts goes on to tell us that Paul spent three months on Malta and was housed by the local magistrate. When he found out the magistrate's father was ill, Paul prayed for him, God healed him, and then every sick person on the island came to Paul for prayer.

Again, Paul prayed, God healed, and the island erupted with revival. When circumstances looked continually impossible to overcome, grace turned defeat into victory and the threat of death into new life for hundreds.

Now, it would be easy to stop here and say of what happened to Paul, "All's well and in the end; Paul won." But there are two things wrong with that statement: First of all, Paul's story wasn't over; and second of all, Paul didn't win in the end. The battle wasn't won at the end—the victory only manifested at this point. The victory was actually won in the midst of the storm.

In all that Wendy and I had been through, from the death of our baby to our bank's agreement to settle with us, I realized that Paul's victory didn't occur when the ship's crew finally saw land. It didn't come when Paul had paddled up onto the beach. It didn't come after he shook off the snake. Paul's victory came in the middle of the storm when he prayed and God answered:

> "For there stood by me this night an angel of the God to whom I belong and whom I serve, saying, 'Do not be afraid, Paul; you must be brought before Caesar; and indeed God has granted you all those who sail with you.' Therefore take heart, men, for I believe God that it will be just as it was told me."
>
> *Acts 27:23-25*

Victory came when Paul decided to bow his knee and seek God's face above all else, even though circumstances appeared grim. It happened when Paul clung to a beam of the ship as it was tossed to-and-fro by the waves. Every detail screamed, "Less!" But God's Spirit said, "I am *more!*"

Paul's victory came in choosing to seek God rather than giving in to defeat. Paul held on until he

> **Every detail screamed, "Less!" But God's Spirit said, "I am more!"**

heard from heaven, and once heaven told him it was done, as far as Paul was concerned, he was already safe and sound, no matter what the storm threw at him.

Jesus is our Deliverer and Savior, but on the night He was to be betrayed, He didn't tell the disciples they had smooth sailing ahead. He told them to ready themselves for the worst. He told them, "'*A servant is not greater than his master.' If they persecuted Me, they* [the world] *will also persecute you*" (John 15:20).

Before He prayed one last time for them, He also said, "*These things I have spoken to you, that in Me you may have peace. In the world you will have tribulation; but be of good cheer, I have overcome the world*" (John 16:33).

As my wife drove home from church recently, our son BJ complained that his ear hurt. Wendy prayed God would touch his ear, but BJ told her it felt even worse. Frustrated and feeling helpless, she prayed again as BJ started crying because of the pain. Wendy came to the end of her rope, hit the steering wheel with her hand, and cried out, "God, why isn't this working?" BJ sat up, dried his tears, and exclaimed, "Mom! It's gone. The pain is gone!"

I'm not suggesting everyone should hit their steering wheel and expect something miraculous to happen. But some of us need a righteous anger that says either this works, or it doesn't. Either His grace is sufficient—or it isn't. As Scripture prescribes, "*Taste and see that the* LORD *is good. Oh, the joys of those who take refuge in him!"* (Psalm 34:8 NLT). We are to trust God and be the proof of His goodness to everyone around us.

What is *more?* Simply put, Jesus doesn't always come as a get-out-of-jail-free card or a winning lottery ticket. He's not a magic wand or a genie in a bottle. He is a person. He is grace. He is peace. He is perseverance. He is righteousness. He is life. He is perspective. He is love. As He spoke to Isaiah:

> **Jesus doesn't always come as a get-out-of-jail-free card or a winning lottery ticket.**

> For as the heavens are higher than the earth,
> So are My ways higher than your ways,
> And My thoughts than your thoughts.
>
> *Isaiah 55:9*

More is not about every problem simply disappearing, but about the resources to face life's situations in strength and faith, knowing He didn't bring you this far to take you back again. Faith is not what you can do, but what the God of More can do through you.

There Is Always a Rescue Plan

The first books of the Bible reveal how the children of Israel complained even though they had been plucked out of slavery, were loaded down with Egypt's riches, and brought safely through the Red Sea and away from Pharaoh's army. But God didn't bring them through all of that just to let them die in the wilderness or wander around the desert forever.

No, he brought them out to bring them in. He replaced their less with more. If that is true of them, then it is also true for us—those for whom Jesus shed His own blood to save. There is no way God is going to leave us without rescue. Just as with the children of Egypt, He will bring us through the dry, parched desert areas of our lives. He will bring us to the place of blessing and bounty.

Similarly, God didn't set Paul on the journey to Rome just to have him die on Malta. He saw Paul through so he could fulfill his calling and destiny. Jesus didn't take his disciples into the boat to have them drown in the middle of the sea. He saw them through safely to the other side.

> **The *more* of Jesus Christ is the grace to fulfill what you would otherwise be unable to complete on your own.**

The *more* of Jesus Christ is the grace to fulfill what you would otherwise be unable to complete on your own. That's why testimonies are so important. Testimonies renew your perspective and encourage your faith, because if He did it for someone else, He can do it for you. And God definitely plays favorites . . . you are His favorite.

When He looks at you, He doesn't see your failures, shortcomings, and sins—He sees the precious blood His son shed to bring you into relationship with Him. He sees the depth of the price that was paid for you. He sees *grace* covering you. He loves you and wants to move on your behalf. He wants to be *more* to you.

That reminds me of the words of King David:

I bow before your holy Temple as I worship.

I praise your name for your unfailing love and faithfulness;
for your promises are backed
by all the honor of your name.

As soon as I pray, you answer me;
you encourage me by giving me strength.

Every king in all the earth will thank you, LORD,
for all of them will hear your words.

Yes, they will sing about the LORD's ways,
for the glory of the LORD is very great.

Though the LORD is great, he cares for the humble,
but he keeps his distance from the proud.

Though I am surrounded by troubles,
you will protect me from the anger of my enemies.

You reach out your hand,
and the power of your right hand saves me.

The LORD will work out his plans for my life—
for your faithful love, O LORD, endures forever.

Don't abandon me, for you made me.

Psalm 138:2-8 NLT

> **This doesn't mean we're impervious to the question "Why?" But life isn't about the *Why*, it's all about the *Who*.**

God will work out His plan in your life. He will be faithful to develop your character and endurance, and to work through you to be an example to others. This doesn't mean we're impervious to the question "Why?" But one thing I have learned is that life isn't about the Why, it's all about the Who. The "Why?" questions have been asked for centuries, and they will continue to be asked long after we're gone. Asking *Why* may leave us unsatisfied; knowing the *Who* will always leave us completely satisfied.

Because of what Wendy and I experienced, we now possess personal experience with the God of More. Given what we have been through, more people will know the grace of God. The God of More doesn't keep us from the storms and challenges of life, but He does help us count it all joy when we go through trials and tribulations. He is with us in our toughest times, and He refuses to leave no matter what we may say. His grace is sufficient. He always operates on the principle of "more than enough."

I don't know what you may be going through as you have read this book, nor do I know what you may be about to face, but I do know Jesus will see you through it. Jesus has the answer to your dilemma, and that answer is a person—*the* Person, Jesus Christ. The grace of God is none other than Jesus. When He shows up, He makes up the difference, covers the cost, changes the atmosphere.

I can do nothing better than to point you to Him, and let you know that He is the only one who will give you *more* when life wants to give you *less*.

Notes

1 To view a video about Eddie, go to: "Heart Healing," YouTube, uploaded by thechurchlvmedia (August 12, 2008), http://www.youtube.com/watch?v=xmHxgLCs1ss.

2 James Strong, *The Exhaustive Concordance of the Bible*, electronic edition (Ontario: Woodside Bible Fellowship., 1996).

BENNY PEREZ MINISTRIES | BENNYPEREZ.ORG

Benny Perez is a pastor, author and speaker who ministers both locally in the Las Vegas valley as the lead pastor of The Church at South Las Vegas, and across the globe. Known for his unique style of communication, leadership and ministry, Benny Perez has seen countless lives impacted by the gospel of Jesus Christ. The purpose of Benny Perez Ministries is to empower individuals and leaders to live life at a higher level in God by imparting and renewing their passion for Jesus.

To invite Benny Perez to speak at your church or event visit: bennyperez.org/invite

STAY CONNECTED WITH PASTOR BENNY PEREZ:

 @BennyPerez   facebook.com/PastorBennyPerez

Your Journey to More: Study Guide

Chapter One: Storm Clouds

Making It Personal

1. When, in your own life, have you found yourself facing a "Why?" How did you respond?
2. In general, how do you cope when you are having difficulties?
3. Do you feel like you can be honest with God when you pray?

Making It Practical

It's okay to be honest with God. You can confide in Him openly and honestly in your reactions to life. In my struggle, I asked God

"Why?" God did not scold me for questioning my circumstances. Instead, He assured me He was with me.

If you are going through a difficult time right now, take a few moments to be honest with God in prayer. After you've been honest in prayer, write down any thoughts or impressions you have. Keep a journal with your Bible so you can record Scriptures that God encourages you with. Write down the Scriptures that seem to "leap off the page" for you!

Scripture for Reflection

Psalm 142:1-3 NLT

I cry out to the LORD; I plead for the LORD's mercy.

I pour out my complaints before Him and tell Him all my troubles.

When I am overwhelmed,

You alone know the way I should turn.

Chapter Two: When the Storm Hits

Making It Personal

1. Have you ever prayed and felt like the answer was "no?" How did that affect your view of God and His love for you?
2. How have you experienced God's presence in your life? Think of a time when you were aware God was with you or moving on your behalf.
3. How has God's presence in your life affected the direction or course of your life?

Making It Practical

At times, when we ask for something from God—and it doesn't happen, disappointment can set in. But remember-the presence of trouble in our lives does not mean the absence of God! We can still be assured that God is with us, and even though circumstances may not make sense; His Presence with us will carry us through!

Spend a few moments each morning thinking about God and inviting Him into your day. At the end of the day, write down how His Presence was felt or known by you throughout your day.

Scripture for Reflection

Psalm 139:7-10 NKJV
Where can I go from Your Spirit?
Or where can I flee from Your Presence?

If I ascend into heaven, You *are* there;
  If I make my bed in hell, behold, You *are there*.
If I take the wings of the morning,
  And dwell in the uttermost parts of the sea,
Even there Your hand shall lead me,
  And Your right hand shall hold me.

Chapter Three: Feeling the Full Fury

Making It Personal

1. When we read the Scriptures, we can immediately see the outcome of each story. However, if you didn't know the outcome of a Bible story, how would that affect your view of the story?
2. Have you ever thought of biblical characters as regular people? Would you classify people like David, Abraham, Ruth, or Elijah as superheroes or as normal people with supernatural help?
3. How does viewing biblical heroes in this way encourage you in your situations? Is there a person or a story in the Bible you really relate to on a personal level? Who or what story?

Making It Practical

It may feel unusual to relate to people in the Bible on a person-to-person level. Yet, what a relief to realize our Bible heroes were people—just like you and me. They went through difficult things, but God brought them through—sometimes through miraculous interventions and sometimes through grace that caused them to persevere. But God brought them through! And if God did it for them, He will also do it for you and for me.

As you think about who in the Bible you can relate to, write down five similarities you share with someone in the Bible—include at least one very human trait (did they lie? doubt God? etc.). Write down the outcome of their story and then encourage yourself daily with what you've learned.

Scripture for Reflection

John 16:33 NLT

I have told you all this so that you may have peace in Me. Here on earth you will have many trials and sorrows. But take heart, because I have overcome the world.

Chapter Four: Staying with the Ship

Making It Personal

1. Sometimes when life becomes difficult, we just want to pull away and isolate ourselves. Have you ever felt like withdrawing from the "ships" in your life (e.g. relationships, discipleship)?
2. What parts of the "ship" do you find easiest to cling to when you are walking through tough times? What parts are the hardest for you to cling to?
3. What single thing can you do today—right now—to reconnect with a key person or "ship" in your life?

Making It Practical

In Christianity, there's no such thing as a Lone Ranger. As I often say when I'm preaching, even the Lone Ranger had a sidekick in Tonto. God never intended for us to walk through life without the support of other Christ followers, the local church, and the resources God freely gives to help us negotiate this world.

As you reflect on the different areas of the "ship" you can hold to in difficult times, take a few moments to think about how you can stay connected. Take time to worship and have fellowship. Make a decision to stay connected through discipleship. If you are not already connected to a local church, make a plan to start visiting local churches in your area. Ask God to lead you to the right church, and then commit to getting involved by serving and reaching out in friendship.

Scripture for Reflection

Ephesians 4:15-16 ESV

Speaking the truth in love, we are to grow up in every way into Him who is the head, into Christ, from whom the whole body, joined and held together by every joint with which it is equipped, when each part is working properly, makes the body grow so that it builds itself up in love.

Chapter Five: Cold and Rainy

Making It Personal

1. Sometimes it may seem like a bad situation has no end, or it can seem like it's going from bad to worse! Have you ever felt hopeless? Have you found yourself in a situation where it feels like things will never change?
2. What are some areas of joy in your life, and people in your life, who give you hope and help you see the possibility of a brighter future?

Making It Practical

Hope is a critical part of making it through the "less" of life and into the "more" God has destined for you. Without hope, we will give up—and the real tragedy is that we may give up too soon—right before the breakthrough. God's presence and the hope He gives will be like a fire in the midst of any circumstance. Continuing to cultivate God's presence in your life, and friendships with people who also have His presence in their lives, will become like a fire of hope for you when life gets difficult.

Think about the warmth of a fire juxtaposed against the backdrop of a cold, rainy day. Consider those people God has placed in your life that give you that sense of warmth. Make a list of three people you know who seem to exude the warmth of God's presence and hope. Reach out to these friends and make them a priority. If you aren't sure you have these friendships yet, pray now and ask God to bring people into your life who will encourage you.

Scripture for Reflection

Lamentations 3:24-26 NKJV

"The LORD is my portion," says my soul, "Therefore I hope in Him!" The LORD is good to those who wait for Him, to the soul who seeks Him. It is good that one should hope and wait quietly for the salvation of the LORD.

Chapter Six: Calm Within the Storm

Making It Personal

1. I find great comfort in realizing that even if our faith is weak, just like the father who asked Jesus to help his unbelief, God is able to handle our weaknesses. Have you ever felt like you weren't sure you could muster up enough faith for the situation you were facing?

2. Does knowing God is compassionate toward you, even when you're weak, help you draw closer to Him when you are in need?

3. How does the Word of God, and understanding the purposes of God for you help you when you suddenly face an unexpected storm?

4. How does understanding the word "rule" (as being like that of an umpire who decides) help with making decisions and responding to situations in life?

Making It Practical

Allowing the peace of God to rule in our heart in the same capacity as an umpire would decide, determine, direct, or control helps give clarity in our decision-making and in negotiating the ups and downs that life brings. We all know when our hearts and our minds are at peace. There is a calm feeling. Our minds aren't racing. We feel assured. In contrast, when we are considering a decision and that peace seems to leave us, we know we might be heading in the wrong direction. In this process, it becomes evident that the peace of God can serve like a compass—pointing us back to the right decision, attitude, or response.

As you ponder the peace of God, think back to a decision you made that brought you peace. Write down the outcome of that decision. In contrast, think about a time when you may have made a decision that caused you to feel anxious. Write down the outcome of that decision. As you move forward in your relationship with God, journal about your decisions and responses. Make a conscious decision to stay in the peace that God gives you, by praying about decisions, relationships, and needs, and allowing the peace He gives to rule.

Scripture for Reflection

2 Corinthians 13:11 ESV
Finally, brothers, rejoice. Aim for restoration, comfort one another, agree with one another, live in peace; and the God of love and peace will be with you.

Chapter Seven: Feeding the Fire

Making It Personal

1. What are the "sticks" in your life that help you to feed the fire of God?
2. How will the disciplines of "picking up sticks" help you in the difficult times of life? As I related these spiritual habits with the rehearsed, instinctive muscle-memory of athletes, how can you apply this truth to your own daily spiritual life?
3. What are some of the obstacles you may have to be aware of, and possibly battle, to establish these important spiritual habits?

Making It Practical

Daily prayer, Bible reading, worship and other spiritual disciplines do not make us righteous in the eyes of God. Only the blood of Jesus makes us innocent before God. Instead, think of these spiritual disciplines as lifelines in the "game of life." Making a conscious choice to daily feed our spirits when things are feeling normal will be the greatest way we can prepare for the difficult seasons.

Set some reasonable goals for you to establish the daily spiritual disciplines listed above. Start with very attainable time goals. Write down the differences you notice in your outlook on life, after you've established some of these good spiritual habits.

Scripture for Reflection

Psalm 119:105 ESV

Your Word is a lamp to my feet and a light for my path.

Chapter Eight: Snake Bit!

Making It Personal

1. Have you ever been feeding the fire of God in your life, feeling like you're doing everything right, only to have your situation "bite back?" How did you react to this?
2. Have you been unfairly accused or criticized? How did you handle this injustice?
3. Have you been tempted to pull back from people, your pastor, or your church? How did you react?

Making It Practical

At some point, we have to acknowledge there is a real devil, and although he is not responsible for everything, the forces at work for him will get stirred up and react when we are infringing on what he thinks is his territory! The sting of a bite, or the injustice of a false accusation can send us running, but God is our help in these moments, and His promises to us are sure.

If you have found yourself in this kind of situation, and have pulled back, I want to encourage you that you can start feeding the fire again right now! You can change the way you are thinking about the situation—from feeling like a victim to knowing you are an overcomer. You can choose to go back to feeding the fire. Take a few moments to pray and ask God to show you any areas you have pulled back from, and ask Him for wisdom and strength to overcome fear. Give Him time to speak to you and write down any impressions or ideas that come to you as you listen.

Scripture for Reflection

Psalm 121:5-8 NIV

The LORD watches over you

> The LORD is your shade at your right hand;

The sun will not harm you by day,

> Nor the moon by night.

The LORD will keep you from all harm—

> He will watch over your life;

The LORD will watch over your coming and going

> Both now and forevermore.

Chapter Nine: Shake It Off!

Making It Personal

1. Have you ever felt tempted to stop doing the right thing (like tithing) when times were difficult? How did you handle the urge to quit? Does pressure change your life strategies positively or negatively?
2. Do people's opinions of you affect how you make decisions?
3. Paul's confidence in God was unwavering even in great difficulties. What is the greatest source of your confidence? From whom or what do you draw strength?

Making It Practical

It's unlikely that you or I will be bitten by a snake in our lifetime. If it were to happen, my natural reaction would be panic! Spiritually, however, we may all face a "snake bite" to varying degrees. We can watch Paul's reaction and think, "I could never keep my composure and just shake it off in such an extreme situation." But here is *the* game-changing truth: the presence of grace—the person of Jesus Christ—makes the impossible possible. God's presence in your life will tip the scales in your favor and empower you in ways you never thought possible; to do things you could never do apart from Him!

One of the greatest keys to God moving in our lives comes through surrender. When we come to the place where we surrender to God in our situation, trust in Him and His word, stop trying to figure out all the whys, and simply receive the Who, we truly encounter the God of More. Take a few moments right now to verbalize fresh surrender to God in the midst of your circumstances, and to say to Him that you trust Him. Even if you aren't sure you can fully let go, take a step of faith. As you pray and surrender to Him, you will find grace.

Scripture for Reflection

Hebrews 4:16 NKJV

Let us therefore come boldly to the throne of grace, that we may obtain mercy and find grace to help in time of need.

Chapter Ten: The Malta Moment

Making It Personal

1. As you have read and reflected on both my story and yours, how has the revelation of the God of More shifted your perspective about your situation?

2. Paul's victory was won when he believed the word of God about his situation and chose to trust what God was saying over what he was seeing. What has God spoken to you about your situation? In what ways can you continue to elevate God's perspective and God's word over your circumstances?

Making It Practical

As we bring our journey together through this book to a close, I want to encourage you. No matter what you are going through, whatever you do, don't give up! God loves you and God is for you. He cannot turn His back on you because He put all of your mistakes on His own son Jesus, so that you could become His child. He will never give up on you—so no matter what you are going through, don't give up on Him!

Prayer of Salvation

I would not want to end this book without giving you the opportunity to receive Jesus as your personal Lord and Savior. We were always meant to walk with God and to be in friendship with Him. If you've never received Jesus or if you feel you are far from Him, pray this prayer:

God, I admit that I have sinned and that I need your forgiveness. Right now, I invite You, Jesus, into my heart and into my life. I ask that You would forgive me. I acknowledge that You are Lord, and I open my heart and my life to you. Be my Lord and Savior and help me as I walk with You. Fill me with your Holy Spirit. In Jesus' name, amen.

If you prayed that prayer for the first time, we want to hear from you! Please send me your testimony via our website at themorebook.com.

Scripture for Reflection

Romans 8:31-32 MSG
So, what do you think? With God on our side like this, how can we lose? If God didn't hesitate to put everything on the line for us, embracing our condition and exposing himself to the worst by sending His own Son, is there anything else He wouldn't gladly and freely do for us?

Postscript

Just as this book was "about to be born" at the printing press, our family received some wonderful news: A one-year-old girl named Bébé was available for adoption placement, and we are just beginning the process. God has given us more than we expected or imagined. What a fitting ending—or comma, really—to our ongoing journey: When life seems to bring a "period," God can indeed insert a "comma" as His love continues to write our story.

Bébé, though the body of this book was already on press when we received the wonderful news of your placement in our family, we dedicate the next book to you—whatever that will be!

In gratitude,
Benny and Wendy Perez

Thoughts and Reflections

Thoughts and Reflections

Thoughts and Reflections

Thoughts and Reflections

Thoughts and Reflections

Thoughts and Reflections

Thoughts and Reflections

Thoughts and Reflections

Thoughts and Reflections

Thoughts and Reflections

Thoughts and Reflections